Praise for Sarah Myers McGinty and The College Application Essay

"If you're worried about your application essay, grab this book."

— *F. Sheppard Shanley, Senior Associate Director of Admission, Northwestern University*

"Sarah McGinty's clear explanation of the role of the college essay in selective admission decisions is right on. Her insight about its impact on candidates is reassuring for students and parents alike."

— *Audrey Smith, Associate Vice President for Enrollment, Smith College*

"Every senior needs two things for a successful college search: a dynamite essay and confidence. This book delivers both."

— *Lindsay Grimm, Princeton graduate*

"Dr. McGinty's book is a must-have on the shelf of every college applicant. It provides just the right amount of information, direction, and encouragement that a student needs to get from vague idea to finished product."

— *Susan Paton, College Counselor, The Hopkins School, New Haven, CT*

"An invaluable how-to manual, written with authority and humor by the reigning expert on this topic ... the definitive book on the college application essay."

— *Carl Bewig, Former Director of College Counseling, Phillips Academy, Andover, MA*

"Sarah McGinty is the dean of writers on college application essays. Any student facing those daunting application questions can profit from reading her book. She is smart and humane."

— *Jon Reider, College Counselor, University High School of San Francisco, CA*

"This book was pivotal in helping me get accepted ..."

— *Brian Prokes, University of Florida graduate*

"Sarah McGinty is my expert extraordinaire when it comes to writing the college essay. Her advice is always clear, concise and right on the mark."

— *Michael Muska, Dean of College Relations, Poly Prep Country Day School, Brooklyn, NY*

"An invaluable resource for students, parents, and counselors…a down-to-earth guide to this anxiety-producing part of the admission process."

— *Scott White, Director of Guidance, Morristown High School, NJ*

"This book transformed my daughter's expectations and therefore her performance. Brilliant!"

— *Sally Guthrie, Parent*

"This book has helped me design my classes."

— *Linda Barrows, English Faculty, The Blake School, Minneapolis, MN*

The College Application *Essay*

Sarah Myers McGinty

The College Application *Essay*

Sarah Myers McGinty

Sixth Edition

The College Board
New York

The College Board

The College Board is a mission driven not-for-profit organization that connects students to college success and opportunity. Founded in 1900, the College Board was created to expand access to higher education. Today, the membership association is made up of over 6,000 of the world's leading educational institutions and is dedicated to promoting excellence and equity in education. Each year, the College Board helps more than seven million students prepare for a successful transition to college through programs and services in college readiness and college success — including the SAT® and the Advanced Placement Program®. The organization also serves the education community through research and advocacy on behalf of students, educators and schools.

For further information, visit www.collegeboard.org.

In all of its book publishing activities the College Board endeavors to present the works of authors who are well qualified to write with authority on the subject at hand and to present accurate and timely information. However, the opinions, interpretations and conclusions of the authors are their own and do not necessarily represent those of the College Board; nothing contained herein should be assumed to represent the official position of the College Board or any of its members.

Copies of this book are available from your local bookseller or may be ordered from College Board Publications, P.O. Box 4699, Mount Vernon, IL 62864. The price is $15.99.

Editorial inquiries concerning this book should be directed to The College Board, 250 Vesey Street, New York, NY 10281.

ISBN: 978-1-4573-0428-6

Printed in the United States of America

Distributed by Macmillan

For John

Contents

Acknowledgments

For anyone who has studied and taught English, writing a book is a wonderfully humbling experience. There is, of course, what Matthew Arnold called "the best that is known and thought in the world," the entire history of British and American literature, with which to compare one's effort. And then there were all the teachers, colleagues, officemates, and mentors (including my eleventh-grade English teacher, a history teacher whose classes were said to embody the charm and wit of a good dinner party, and a marathon-running vice principal) who have preceded me, shared with me, and inspired me. And last, there are the best teachers in the world, my students. Writing this book meant continual collision with something learned from someone else. I acknowledge and thank all these sources, especially my students, and most particularly my Millburn High School students. Of all who passed through room 210, it was the one in the front of the class who learned the most and had the most fun!

I also want to thank those who have guided this book to publication — Eric Rayman in particular — as well as those involved in college admission — counselors, staffers and applicants — who shared with me their writing, their experiences, and their insights. Dodge Johnson, Michael Muska, Rick Rizoli, and Scott White contributed expertise and editorial advice. Claire Garpestad, Jackie Lebovitz, John Snow, and Jack Stubbs shared their work. Tara Dowling, Lisa Ratmansky and Susan Paton were indispensable Tiggers to my Eeyore. Thanks also to Sutton Trust, to NACAC, and to Harvard University for their research support.

— S. M. M.

Chapter 1

How Colleges Read Applications

"The essay is the first thing I read. I really slow down over that," says Thyra Briggs, vice president and dean of admission at Harvey Mudd College. Briggs is acknowledging the importance of the essay in differentiating applicants. "A picture of the student begins there," she adds. Of course, as in all admission offices, the transcript is the primary source of information about an applicant. But after that, when admission counselors want a sense of the person behind the paper, when they are looking for the match between institution and applicant, essays can make the case. "A great essay can close the deal," says Briggs. "It's the one place to clearly hear the student's voice."

Harvey Mudd's process is its own, but it is not entirely different from that of other colleges. In most admission offices, grades, and courses — the transcript — are where evaluation begins. Then other factors are taken into account: talents, recommendations, activities, testing, special circumstances, a portfolio or supplemental materials, an audition, an interview. Woven into all this is an interest in the applicant's personality and writing ability. The application essay gives colleges useful information about both of these features.

Where It All Began

The application essay or personal statement has been a part of college admission since the explosion of college enrollment after World War II, evolving from direct queries like "Why in particular do you wish to attend Bates?" to more eccentric requests like "Your favorite word" (Princeton University) or "What activities make you lose track of time?" (Mount Holyoke College). The Reverend Robert Kinnally, former dean of admission at Stanford University, believes the essay helps admission counselors "judge the depth of the [applicant's] understanding of intellectual or social issues ... it also shows the quality and freshness of the applicant's mind." Although not every college requires an application essay, narrative prose figures into the admission process at a wide variety of institutions — for the 38,000 applicants to the University of Michigan, for the 35,000 applicants to Harvard University, for the 12,000 applicants to the United States Military Academy at West Point, and for the 1,600 applicants to Carroll College in Helena, Montana. The evaluation of the essay may contribute to how a college differentiates among its top applicants. Or it may determine whether a borderline candidate has the necessary basic skills. Colleges use essays for different purposes, but essays matter — at large, small, public, private, selective, and nonselective schools.

How Colleges Read Essays

Colleges are looking to build scholarly communities, hoping to collect a population of people who like to read and think, reflect and talk, wonder and argue. This is the mission of admission. But as William C. Hiss, former dean of admission at Bates College, says, "We are often seen, wrongly, I think, as a set of intellectual gatekeepers who, like Dante's *Divine Comedy*, offer three possibilities: paradise, purgatory or hell — that is, admit, wait-list, deny." In contrast, the colleges themselves see a methodical and quantifiable process of selection. Marlyn E. McGrath, director of admission at Harvard University, describes the admission staff as a group of hard-working people "determined to bring to Harvard students who are diverse in talents and interests." In choosing a class of first-year students, admission counselors make judgments that involve objective information (comparing two students' course loads, for example) and subjective information (a coach's opinion about how far a specific player might develop within the college's tennis program). It's what Fred Hargadon, former dean of admission at Princeton, liked to call "precision guesswork."

Making Choices

The anxiety about all this, for high school students and their families, is very real. And it's easy to start believing that the college admission process is going to be the most significant and determining feature in a young person's life. (Actually, what you do in college is more important than where you go to college.) But the "big picture" isn't a pattern of injustice and irrationality. Both colleges and applicants are looking and choosing. Both admission counselors and high school seniors are busy gathering information and making judgments based on facts and predictions. In pursuit of a common goal — the best education of the next generation of leaders and thinkers — colleges and universities, like you, will look at many options.

Your research probably started first and you have many resources to draw upon:

- Guidance personnel and the counseling and career staff at your high school and at your local library
- Websites, social media, mailings, videos, blogs and viewbooks from the colleges
- Admission counselors — at the colleges, visiting at your high school, or at local-area information fairs
- Teachers, coaches, educational consultants, friends, parents, alumni (preferably recent alumni)
- Guidebooks and data handbooks
- Campus visits and interviews
- Prior applicants from your own high school or community
- Word of mouth, general reputation, and media coverage (not the most reliable information)

You aren't doing this alone. All these resources will help you with your half of the choosing — deciding where to apply to college. Colleges rely on a more focused set of resources:

- Course of study

- Grades, class rank, and grade point average

- Test scores

- Biographical data (summer activities, jobs, special talents, and interests)

- One or more essays, writing samples, or paragraph responses

- Support materials where appropriate (audition, tapes, portfolio)

- Recommendations

- An interview when available

Inside the Admission Office

Let's look at how colleges make their decisions, in order to understand where the application essay fits into the picture.

The evaluation process differs at every school. Some colleges see numerical data as the most reliable predictor of success: They look first at an applicant's grades, class rank, and test scores. The state of California, for example, publishes eligibility minimums and uses a variety of criteria for each of its different UC campuses. Other schools try to tease from the file a richer sense of the applicant. Vince Cuseo, vice president and dean for admission at Occidental College, says, "We read to uncover character, values, and something of the life experience." And where a school offers a distinctive program — the K plan at Kalamazoo College, the internship options at Northeastern, the hands-on education of Deep Springs — application evaluation stresses the "fit" of applicant and education. All schools, even the large state universities, have a special process for the question marks — the "gray zone" applications that may require additional readers or consideration by a committee. Colleges and universities continually modify the way they evaluate applications, looking for the most reliable and the fairest way to put together a class from the limited information provided.

The people who make these decisions also vary. The readers of applications are usually a combination of experienced senior admission personnel and younger staffers, often themselves recent graduates of the school. A dean of admission or an enrollment manager oversees everything. But faculty members may be part of the process. At Cal Tech, all admission decisions involve faculty. Reed College includes student readers on admission committees. Applicants may also be looked at by specialists: music faculty hear auditions, art staff view portfolios. Claudia Harrison, a geography teacher and applications advisor at James Allen's Girls' School in Dulwich, UK, recommends the UCAS website as a useful resource for students as they complete the 47 line (4,000 characters) essay required on the application to universities in the United Kingdom. "These essays are read by admission tutors, scholars who have devoted their lives to a discipline, and they are, quite naturally, looking for achievements and depth of knowledge in that discipline."

The committee is not then a nameless, faceless group of people, uniform in taste and attitude. It is made up of individuals. Assigned seemingly endless files of applications in the dark days of winter, such an audience — overworked and tired — may find that a creative, innovative, interesting or unique element in an application makes the difference. High scores and great grades do stand out. But students mistake their audience when they visualize a stuffy bunch of academics in search of an academic superstar.

Are all applications read in the same way? They can't be. In fact, as Ted O'Neill, former dean of admission at the University of Chicago, points out, "We don't want them all to be read in the same way. A collection of identical people would make a very boring college." So there is no perfect applicant, no "just what they want" that applicants should shape themselves to be. Many things are sought within a class and many different elements make up the admission committee's final judgment. The application is a web of information, a jigsaw puzzle that is interconnected and interactive. Each element plays its own part; each makes its own argument.

Here's what admission will consider:

Your High School Record

The numbers come first. Colleges request grades, usually beginning with ninth grade. (If you have been homeschooled, your supervisor will complete a detailed curriculum report as part of your application.) Three and a half years of performance provides a picture of your academic achievement and also a look at the pattern of your growth and progress. Straight A's are nice — but rare in a challenging course of study. An improvement in grades is positive, too — the opposite will certainly raise eyebrows in the admission office. But above all other factors in the grade pattern, most colleges scrutinize the course load. A grade of B in Advanced Placement® English is more important than an A in chorus. An A in chemistry carries more weight than an A in civics. Grades, class rank and grade point average are viewed in light of your course choices. Some admission offices add a factor to a student's grades for a strong educational program or for more challenging courses — Advanced Placement courses, a math class at the local college, study with a respected voice coach at a conservatory.

Grades, class rank, and grade point average are also viewed in terms of your high school and its student body. Colleges assign regional responsibility to members of the admission staff who familiarize themselves with a few states or with one part of the country. They know each high school and its course offerings. Some secondary schools have a reputation for excellence; others have less rigorous programs. Each school's general quality is considered in evaluating class rank and course of study. So while a B in AP® Physics will count more than an A in Introduction to Science, a B from a renowned application-based high school like Boston Latin School will count for more than an A from a school that just lost its accreditation.

Test Scores

Testing contributes numbers to your application. Many schools require the SAT®, some SAT Subject Tests™, or the ACT. Some applicants may provide Advanced Placement Exam scores; language competency scores from the Test of English as a Foreign Language (TOEFL) or the International English Language Testing System (IELTS); scores from the International Baccalaureate exam (IB); O-Levels; other testing administrated in a home country. These standardized tests help admission personnel evaluate applicants' potential for a successful performance in college. The scores are a yardstick by which students of widely differing backgrounds can be compared. Testing may seem impersonal and "unfair," but it is part of the access path to higher education in every developed country from Beijing to Istanbul, from Edinburgh to Buenos Aires.

The admission committee will look at your scores and compare them to your grades. High grades can overcome low scores, but admission personnel

will carefully scrutinize the course load and the high school's reputation. High scores can sometimes compensate for low grades, but that particular combination tends to make admission personnel nervous: Does the student lack motivation? Is she just a bright goof-off?

Grades, course load, grade point average, class rank, and scores are the numerical information colleges use to evaluate an application. They look to your past as a clue to your future. Studies show that neither grades nor test scores alone indicate whether an applicant will succeed in college. However, the combination of high school record *and* scores has been found to be a fairly valid indicator of college success. College work also relies on the same study habits, self-discipline, skills, and personal qualities — enthusiasm, organization, independence of thought, responsibility, perseverance — needed in high school. These qualities contribute to success in a career as well.

As you begin to think about college options, keep all your high school numbers in mind. Don't let yourself become overwhelmed by standardized test scores. Remember that the numbers colleges list are often the *median* scores, not the cutoff scores. If a school lists its median SAT math score as 600, then 50 percent of the class scored higher than 600, and 50 percent scored lower. Many schools now list the SAT test score range of the middle 50 percent of the first-year class. The score range of admitted students is often higher than the range for applicants, but in both cases, there are students with scores above and below the given numbers.

Numbers are only part of your application. They will, however, help you determine which schools are your long shots and which are likely to be satisfied with your performance. They will help the admission committee determine if you are a sure accept, a clear deny, or a maybe.

Other sections of the application are less numerical. A long history of research, from work sponsored by the College Board to studies in applied psychology that focus on university admission, hiring practices, and even military and leadership skills, while confirming the validity of testing and grade-point averages as useful in predicting college and career success, has found that personal qualities — from motivation to study habits — figure significantly in performance. Many colleges look to recommendations, essays, and the interview to give them that needed sense of the person. And some colleges consider these elements primary criteria in an admission decision.

Recommendations

Evaluations will be written by your high school counselor and by a few of your teachers. Make these most effective by scheduling an early appointment with your counselor to discuss your college selection. If your high school is large, your relationship with your counselor may be a bit remote. The national ratio of students to counselors is 460:1, but recent U.S. Department of Education data found a broad range from 814:1 in Arizona to 197:1 in Wyoming. You might want to prepare a simple life history or a resume for your counselor. It's good preparation for filling out the applications and, by listing some of your circumstances and activities, you help your counselor write a specific and informed recommendation.

Approach your teachers early. Ask for recommendations from teachers who like you, with whom you have done well, whose courses relate to your intended area of specialization, and who are themselves articulate, careful, and responsible. You want a positive letter and one that will be consistent with the rest of your application. But don't forget that such a letter isn't likely to be written by even your favorite teacher if he or she is overworked, hassled and pressed for time. Ask, "Do you have the time to write a recommendation for me? I'm looking at Wesleyan, Oberlin and Sarah Lawrence." Name the schools, as that will guide the response. And don't be downcast if the teacher says he or she is too busy or can't do it. Approach someone else. You don't want your request gathering dust on the "to-do list" of a teacher who meant to do it but had too many periods of cafeteria duty to find the time.

You might want to give the teachers your brief resume. They will rely mostly on what you've done in their classes, but it helps if they know you were entering piano competitions or working nights at McDonald's while you were turning out first-rate reports on Jacksonian democracy. Give the recommending teacher a list of the courses you took with him or her, the grades you received, and any special projects or major papers you wrote. Students come and go and most teachers appreciate a little memory jogging. Your teacher will probably upload her recommendation after receiving an email notification initiated by you through the Common Application website. Or she may submit the letter through your school's Naviance system. Waive your right of access; it shows confidence in your recommender and adds credibility to the letter. Thank-you notes at the end of the process are appropriate.

The Interview

The interview is no longer as common as the large-group information session, but if you have the opportunity, whether on campus or with a local alumni interviewer, go into an interview with a specific sense of what you want to emphasize about yourself and with a set of questions about the school that are not answered on the website.

Creating that resume will help you with questions about your academic career and activities. Interview questions may be similar to those asked on the application, so review or complete your application before the interview. Review the "idea bank" you will create in Chapter 4 as another preparation. It helps to have one interview at a college that is a "likely"; you need to feel needed at about this time. Schedule the most important interview late in the sequence; you'll be more experienced and confident.

Do your "homework" and use the interviewer's knowledge of the college to help you get to know the school better. One applicant advised, "I tried to go into the interviews with an open mind and roll with the punches. But I had questions ready, too. When the alumni interviewer from Yale asked, 'Why Yale?' I asked 'What made you go here?'" The better your questions, the better the impression you will make and the more useful the interview will be. Questions about the social life or how many students stay on campus during the weekend are better asked during the campus tour. Make your questions genuine. It's much better to ask "Would you send your child to this school?" than "Do you have a major in computer science?" The interview is a two-way street, not just an opportunity to impress the admission personnel. Rick Rizoli, long-time director of college counseling at The Rivers School in Weston, MA, reminds students, "You are evaluating them as much as they are evaluating you." Use the interview to assess further the fit between you and the school, to learn if *you* want to choose *them*.

The interview is rarely required and not every school uses the interview to evaluate an applicant. Sometimes you have only half an hour to make an impression and gather information, and the first five minutes is spent getting oriented and trying to relax ("Did you find a parking place? How long a drive was it?"). Some interviewers find students too shy or guarded to be accurately assessed in a short, high-pressure meeting. Some alumni interviewers won't be able to answer all your questions, either. But take the chance, at home or on campus, and remember, it's not a performance; it's a resource.

The Essay

Now for the tricky stuff. The numbers are behind you. What you've done in high school is settled. Don't expend energy or worry over things you can't change: the school you attended, the C+ in English 11. There are grades to be earned for the senior year and this is certainly no time to coast. But most of the numbers your high school will send to the colleges are fixed. Your recommendations are in the works. The last part of your evaluation will be drawn from the essay.

Not every college asks for an essay. But it is required on the Common Application, a form accepted by more than 500 colleges. And it is an option at many more schools. It may be required of transfers or the applicant applying to a special program or honors curriculum. Filling even a small text box for "Which of your extracurricular activities has had the most meaning for you?" can require all the skills (and yield most of the information) of a full-length essay.

One underlying assumption made by admission offices that ask for an essay is that a student's writing will tell them something about a student's writing ability. That makes sense. Organization, usage, and correctness count. In addition, colleges believe that a student's writing will tell them something about the student's personality, thought process, values, preferences, and style. So content counts, too. Scott White, legendary director of guidance at Morristown High School in New Jersey, notes, "A lot of schools really do value good writing and want to get a sense of who the student is." The essay is important both for how it's written and for what it's written about. *Can you write? Can you think? What do you care about?*

Colleges weigh these questions — and the essay that reflects them — with varying degrees of emphasis. Where grades in English or test scores raise questions about writing ability, the essay will be carefully reviewed. Where the transcript and support documents fail to provide a strong sense of the applicant's passions and enthusiasms, the essay may fill in the blanks. For liberal arts majors applying to Connecticut College, director of admission Deborah Wright points out that the essay ranks second only to performance in the high school course program in the application review.

Even when the essay isn't among the top three or four factors in the evaluation of an applicant, it may surface in "gray zone" cases, where a clear judgment about the applicant hasn't emerged from several reviews of the application. Admission counselors may connect to a student who has intrigued them with thoughts about Cuban independence or missing sweat socks or Coach Pike; such connections can tip the balance on the last day.

Can You Write?

Combined with your English grades and some test scores, the application essay reveals your writing abilities — organization, analysis, interpretation — and your mastery of the conventions of standard written English. You'll need all this in college. As further information on the same subject, some applications require an essay prepared and graded as a classroom assignment. A graded school paper can reveal both the skill of the writer and the level of expectation at the secondary school. Wheaton (MA), Sarah Lawrence, Hampshire, Bennington and Ursinus are among the schools that ask for this supplementary material. David Wagner, associate dean at Hampshire, notes: "It's one of the most useful things we have; student writing confirms everything else in the file."

Because your ability to interpret, analyze, and express yourself clearly, correctly and vividly will be crucial in your college courses, your application essay will be looked at in these same terms. Consider it a chance to make an important claim (in this case, the claim is "Pick me!") and be persuasive about it. Give yourself enough time to do a thorough and careful job. Tell your own story. Don't try to sound like Albert Einstein or David Foster Wallace. Get some feedback in the thinking stages from a teacher, parent, or school counselor. Then polish, spell-check and proofread. Admission counselors remember — but not necessarily with affection — essays like the one that ended, "And from that day, Daniel was my best fried."

Can You Think?

In addition, admission committees use the essay to get to know the student in a more specific and personal way than the numbers and recommendations provide. Laura McPhie Oliveira, former vice president for enrollment management at Salve Regina University, says, "So much is just a matter of numbers. The essay is where the student has to slow down, reflect. It's still the only time where they speak for themselves."

Nancy Siegel, long-time director of guidance at Millburn High School in New Jersey, agrees: "Colleges want a third dimension. Without the essay, the application profile is flat." Even Brigham Young University, with a fairly homogeneous applicant pool, finds diversity in the essays. The university asks applicants why they have chosen a school within the Latter-Day Saints educational system; since most applicants are members of the Church of Jesus Christ of Latter-Day Saints, one might expect a fairly uniform response. But their dean noted, "Although all our applicants say they want to come to BYU for the education and for the right spiritual atmosphere, this is said in many different ways. The essay can tell us about the thought process, the maturity of thinking, purposes, and goals." Clearly, each application is a jigsaw puzzle and each part contributes a piece to the overall picture.

What Do You Care About?

How does this puzzle work? Choice is important. The process of choosing an answer, and often a question, is central to all college essays. Choice shows something about what and how you think, about what you value within a set of choices; it can show priorities, preferences, and even a bit about your judgment. The applicant whose "local issue" is the need for more student parking at the high school is both a little similar and also rather different from the applicant who is concerned about the homogeneous composition of the town planning board. Nancy Donehower, director of college counseling at the Catlin Gabel School and former dean of admission at Reed College, in Portland, Oregon, says, "If he says his summer in France taught him to observe cultural differences, and then says, 'For example, in France the cars are a lot smaller,' this gives a good idea of how little he's thought about and analyzed his life experiences."

The essay adds a personal, human element to the application. It can breathe life into your activities, interests, experiences, or family situation, making these elements real and vivid. Donehower adds, "For me, reading at Reed, the essay was the most important part of the application. For a small college with a personal approach rather than an 'acceptability quotient,' it was the place where the kids would strut their stuff. It tells a lot about character. It can reveal the person who likes to learn because she likes learning or the person who finds the process greater than the product."

A Few Red Flags

- The essay should not be an explanation of grades or exceptional circumstances in your background. If your grades and scores are not reflective of your ability, if your numbers don't tell all, the essay is, of course, another chance to shine. And if there are very special circumstances in your life — an illness, a family situation, a handicap — be sure to tell the college about this in a separate statement. Submit a brief account of this subject whether it's asked for or not (the Common Application offers a place for such additional information right after the essay: "Please provide an answer below if you wish to provide details of circumstances or qualifications not reflected in the application.") But don't make this story your core essay.

- The essay should add — add substantially — to the application. Don't default to a predictable, prepackaged sentiment. "I chose X College because X is committed to learning and I want to learn." Oh dear, I think that's rather a given, isn't it? These are academic institutions you are applying to and while there are parties every weekend, there are also a lot of classes to be passed. "I want to give as much to X as I know X will give to me." Nice parallelism in that sentence but not much basis yet for such an assertion. Probably better to name a course you plan to take. And do take it seriously. Dartmouth once asked applicants to create an ideal application question and answer it; they did not learn much from questions like "Are you having a nice day?" and they stopped laughing after the second hundred set of responders asked "Will I be admitted" and then wrote "Yes." Don't be completely afraid of a risk: "These are the voyages of the Starship Nussbaum." But get a second opinion on any essay or response driven by your idea of your wonderful sense of humor. Get several opinions on that YouTube clip you're planning to attach; if you go through with it, use a privacy setting and provide the access code with your link.

- Reading essay drafts, Rick Rizoli at The Rivers School says, "I ask myself, 'Does this connect to everything else in the application? Does this sound like the kid?'" The essay should be you, in your words. Don't outsource this to a parent or professional and don't download it from the Internet. Admission people can tell. They've spent a little time on the Internet themselves. They have bloggers in the office and a Facebook page for the school. They've seen the "… but I've never gone to college" essay thousands of times. And they will mark your essay "DDI" if they conclude "Daddy did it."

Summary

Success at any school depends on knowing what you're in for; nothing is more bitter than disappointed expectations. The essay is particularly useful in determining the fit between the applicant and the college. David Wagner at Hampshire, says, "Our students design their own programs through negotiation with faculty advisers. We need to be sure they have the motivation and vision to do that. The essay is one of the places we look for confirmation." If a college has a particular character — its curriculum is tightly focused (Fashion Institute of Technology, the U.S. service academies) or it relies on a special calendar (Colorado College's block plan), teaching methodology (Sarah Lawrence College) or curriculum (St. John's great books program), the essay can reflect an understanding of and enthusiasm for this special setting.

The recommendations are always positive and the interview is becoming less common and more a momentary "snapshot." But like the moment in *The Wizard of Oz* when the screen goes from black and white to color, the essay can light up and personalize your self-presentation. It is the one aspect of the application process that is entirely open to development and safely in your hands. It is an opportunity to show the admission committee a little about yourself, your insights, your enthusiasm, and your writing ability. The essay is also an opportunity to convey, under less pressure and with more preparation than the interview, something of your personal style; it counteracts the numbers and the anonymity of the application process.

Clearly, the essay adds to the overall pattern of your application. The colleges take it seriously; you should too. It is part of your need to compete and the college's need to select. "The essay can be a powerful 'tipper' in close cases, especially with very strong or very poor essays," says Bates' Bill Hiss. If an essay is required or even allowed, use it to present yourself effectively. Remember, it is a separate part of the application and should convey information not found elsewhere. If you ignore this advice, you defeat the college's purpose in requesting an essay. Seize this opportunity to stand out from the better numbers, the similar recommendations, and the other kids. Don't default on it; don't give it away. It's a wonderful opportunity to speak out for yourself in that remote, fluorescent maze of little offices. It's not so terrible and it's not so hard. You've actually already done plenty of writing like this!

Toolbox: A Timeline for Applying to College

Freshman Year

- With your parents and your school counselor, plan a college preparatory academic program for all four years of high school.

- Make friends in the guidance office.

- Take SAT Subject Tests relevant to your course selections.

- Find out your school code or CEEB number.

Sophomore Year

- Take any testing relevant to your course selections.

- Begin researching the application process if you are interested in Division I or II athletic requirement or a U.S. military service academy; the experience, deadlines, and requirements will be substantially different.

- Look for a summer program, camp, volunteer opportunity or job related to your areas of interest — do something constructive and/or interesting with your summer.

Junior Year

- Visit college fairs; meet with college representatives who visit your school; talk to friends and alumni; look at various college websites; ask counselors and teachers for suggestions.

- Meet with your school counselor and, with your parents, develop a list of colleges of interest. Think about high school: What have you liked and what would you like to change? College is more school; try to make it more school of the kind you favor.

- Find some online or school-supplied interest inventories to help you choose potential college majors or careers.

- Talk to your parents about the finances. Is there a maximum your family can afford to pay? Ask guidance for samples of financial aid forms and for local scholarship options. Ask a parent to fill out financial aid estimates (these appear on college websites).

- If you want to play Division I or II athletics, talk to your coach and counselor about the NCAA Eligibility Center requirements.

- Take the PSAT/NMSQT° in October. Schedule the ACT or SAT; your school counselor will help you time this well.

- Do some Web research of class listings or read students' blogs at the schools that interest you. You will need some depth of knowledge of your specific interests — e.g., is their psychology department behavioral or humanistic? Does the linguistics department favor structural linguistics or sociolinguistics? Is rowing a sport or a club? Does the *a cappella* choir require sight-reading auditions?

- Take SAT Subject Tests if any colleges on your list require them. Take AS level exams (UK), IB, or Advanced Placement exams at the end of the appropriate course of study.

- Visit colleges in the spring when students are there; many colleges do not interview applicants until after March of their junior year.

- Near the end of the year, ask recent teachers to write your recommendations. Draft a brief resume, especially if you have a special talent or extensive athletic involvement.

- Deepen extracurricular involvements.

- Keep a journal or collect interesting "important moment" articles from your reading as samples for your essay. See the guide to an "idea bank" in Chapter 4.

- Schedule the strongest senior course program you can handle. Unless you have good reason not to, include all five academic areas: English, math, science, languages, and social studies or history. The idea is depth of study rather than a smattering of everything.

- Register on your school's Naviance site if this is used by your guidance office. Include your parents in discussions of the information you find there.

- Save some of your best class work. You might offer a paper, lab, or small portfolio to the teachers who write your recommendations. And some colleges ask for a graded paper as part of your application.

- Summer: Build on interests and commitments you have already identified. Don't look for a new "vaccination" of something you think the college wants to see. Stick with your interests and expand them. Get a job if you can. Consider drafting a couple of rough versions of application essays. And the Common Application website will be up and renewed in August. Complete the easy parts and save; it will make your Mom happy.

Senior Year

September

- Focus on your classes and do well in them.

- Meet with your school counselor to discuss your college choices and timing; present your tentative list of colleges and ask, "What am I missing? What looks like a good match to you?"

- Continue campus visits and interviews. Whenever possible, visit on ordinary days for "business as usual" and on choreographed "prospective student" days for a lot of information in a compressed format.

- Line up your recommending teachers.

- File the NCAA Eligibility Center forms if you plan to play Division I or II sports.

- Preregister for the CSS/Financial Aid PROFILE® if required by any of your colleges (www.collegeboard.com/css).

- If applying Early Decision or Early Action, or to a college with rolling admission, write your application and the necessary essays. Or if ED and EA aren't in the plan, pull together in one file all or most of the essay topics. There should be overlap in the supplements and you will want time for your ideas to develop.

October

- Confirm your list of college choices with your counselor. Decide if you will apply regular decision or by one of the early deadlines (see individual college options).

- Enroll recommending teachers in Naviance or on the Common Application website (the latter generates an email from which they can submit their letters). You may want to give them your resume. You will definitely want to drop them a thank-you note after the deadlines.

- Take the SAT test and any necessary SAT Subject Tests.

- Group Common Application schools together and download all the required supplements from the Common Application website: http://www.commonapp.org. Look for logical recycling opportunities (except for the "why us" question) and the possibility that the main Common Application essay might serve you for the essay required at a non-Common Application school. Begin drafting responses.

- Research scholarships that may apply to you. Make sure you and your parents are in agreement about college finances.

- Complete any rolling admission applications, particularly to those state institutions that require only a transcript, an application form, and test scores. Remember, however, that no application is read until it's complete, so be sure all your pieces are submitted on time.

November

- If you are applying for financial aid, use the Free Application for Federal Student Aid (FAFSA) forms. Your parents will fill out the FAFSA online at www.fafsa.ed.gov.

- If you are applying for scholarships, don't think you need to pay for searching or advice. The information on all programs is free — it just requires time to do the research and courage to make the applications.

- There may be more SAT tests and/or SAT Subject Tests to complete.

- Early Decision and Early Action deadlines are in October and November. Remember that you can make only one Early Decision application (you will sign an Early Decision agreement form), and you are bound to attend if that school admits you. Some colleges also offer nonbinding Early Action. But let your school counselor know exactly what you are planning so every feature of the plan you are applying under is well understood by you, your counselor, and your parents.

- Even if you are applying Early Decision, you need to begin filling out applications and writing essays for the Regular Decision deadlines (see Chapter 5). You may not need to send more applications if your Early dream comes true. But if it doesn't, you will want to head into the winter break confident that you've completed the work for your other applications. Most Regular deadlines will fall between December 1 and February 15.

December

- You may want to take additional SAT tests or SAT Subject Tests.

- Upload your final work. Most colleges want you to apply entirely online; some will waive the application fee if you do.

- Proofread everything TWICE!

- Make a checklist to be sure you've had scores sent, paid the fee, and notified your counselor about each school you're applying to. Hit "send" before any midnight deadlines (and they aren't always at midnight) — you don't want to be caught in a server crash. Try to use whatever means the school provides to verify receipt of online material; there is an automatic notification with Common Application submissions.

January—March

- Follow up on any missing details; continue to submit applications according to the deadlines.

- Focus on producing a solid senior record; it's your last chance to "rule the school."

- Your "demonstrated interest" is a factor. Continue to visit or interview if you missed a school of interest; it's best, however, to do this before they act on your application. Some schools with rolling admission accept applications well into the spring.

- If you are applying for aid, prepare and file financial aid forms (www. FAFSA.ed.gov) and other scholarship applications. Check deadlines and priority dates for each of your colleges.

April—June

- When your letters come through, expect at least one denial. It's probably going to be part of the process somewhere along the way and it only shows you've measured correctly the full range of your own possibilities.

- Don't run down the halls shouting, "I got in." If you want to celebrate, make it a private affair.

- Revisit the colleges that have admitted you and that are "finalists" on your list. Touring a school when you know you can enroll there is very enlightening. Ask yourself, "Is this where I want to take my talents and charms? Can these people be my friends?"

- Review your financial aid offers as part of this reevaluation and selection process.

- Choose one school and make your deposit before the universal reply date of May 1.

- If you choose to remain on a waiting list, send a letter expressing your interest and any new information that might strengthen your case. Keep in close contact with your school counselor to understand how and when wait-listed candidates are reconsidered.

- If you can find one, get a summer job that pays good money.

- Think about taking a "gap year." Travel? Study abroad? Work for AmeriCorps? Most colleges will let you defer one year. But don't get drawn into this idea too deeply until you've completed a successful application process within the support system of your high school.

- Go to the prom, even if you have to go with your cousin.

Sometimes I think students devote their senior summer to making home a place they are willing to leave. But thank your parents for all they've done for you at some point before you pack your bags; recognize that the big scary change in your life is mirrored by a big scary change in theirs.

Chapter 2

You've Done This Before

The essay is a special opportunity to introduce yourself. "This is a time to engage with the people who are making the decisions," says Curtis Rodgers, dean of enrollment management at Columbia University School of General Studies. You have an attentive audience that believes this part of your application will give useful additional information, a different and reliable lens on you. And although the admission committee will not choose or reject you on the basis of this single element, the essay can be a strong voice in your favor, a way to stand out from the rest, a determining factor for a "gray zone" application. According to Audrey Smith, associate vice president for enrollment at Smith College, "We'll take a risk for the right reason." Sometimes it is the essay that gives them that reason. So while admission people want to hear from your high school counselors and teachers, they also want to hear from you.

The Challenge of the College Essay

The college essay is, in one way or another, an essay of analysis. What makes it tricky is that, in this case, it's self-analysis. Self-analysis, objective judgment about your own actions, is not easy; it can be especially hard to do at this point in your life, when many of your goals and plans are unsettled. You may already have confronted this problem at an interview. Admission people ask, "What are you interested in?" or "What are your hopes and aspirations?" These are questions that require self-analysis, and they're pretty hard. The college has questions about you partly because you still have questions about yourself. But the essay is a chance to demonstrate which questions you've asked yourself and what answers you've found.

The college, then, is asking you to do something genuinely difficult — tell about yourself — and here the pressure is really on. The audience is critical and crucial; readers unknown to you intend to take your performance seriously.

The essay is also going to be examined as a clue to your writing ability. Northwestern lets you know what they're looking for right on their website: We "read your essays to get a better sense of your interests, thought processes, and writing ability." Andrew Stewart, a high school principal in St. Charles, MO, sees wisdom in this strategy: "Of course the essay is seen as an index to student writing. After all, college work involves a lot of essays, written tests, research write-ups. Skill in essay writing is essential to success in college." In fact, Carol Lunkenheimer, when she was dean and director of admission at Northwestern, looked to the essay as a useful defense of a student's acceptability: "It is greatly in an applicant's favor if the reader can say, 'This kid can write.'"

So the challenge is to have your own say with power and precision. You in one page! Clearly there is pressure here, and it is natural for anything that is challenging to be a little threatening. But with yourself as the subject, you actually have all it takes to succeed!

A New but Familiar Assignment

Thinking about applying and actually completing applications are two different matters. It was fun looking at pictures and blogs, reading the course offerings, and fantasizing about next fall. But now the burden of choice is shifting from the schools you choose to the schools that will choose you.

As described in Chapter 1, much of the data for this decision is settled. Grades have been recorded, scores reported, recommendation letters provided. But the essay is yet to be written. The application you're filling out may ask for a list of the items you'd include in a time capsule or perhaps you've decided to describe the influence of your favorite Harry Potter book. Even a straightforward question like "Discuss an accomplishment or event ..." may seem unfamiliar, intimidating, unlike anything you've done before. What kind of event is life-changing? Can it be a lost phone or should global politics be involved? Your teachers assigned papers and reports, with topics such as the theme of love in a particular novel or the causes of a given war. This seems to be a very different business.

But think about it for a moment and you'll realize that you have, in fact, done this assignment before — *many* times. All those papers for English class — and for history, and even for science — were essentially like the college essay. And even if the college essay seems harder, it isn't. It's just different — and in many ways it's easier.

Consider F. Scott Fitzgerald's novel *The Great Gatsby*. You may have read this in an American literature course. And if you did, it would not surprise you if your teacher asked you to look over the novel, choose an element, scene or character, and write a few pages about how this bit figured into the whole. That assignment might have been:

"In three to five paragraphs, show how Gatsby's purchase of the house in West Egg represents his hopeful optimism and can be connected to the hopefulness and dreams of several other characters."

In the case of the application essay, the "text" is you. And the assignment is:

"In three to five paragraphs, tell us about something you've done or thought that will represent both your character and a larger sense of who you are and what you value."

Not that different. Not that unfamiliar. Just challenging because it's you and not Jay Gatsby.

The Structure

A college essay is nothing new; it is the type of writing with which you are most familiar. Let's look at your writing skills and the kind of writing you have learned in the last 12 years.

First of all, it was organized — your paper on *The Great Gatsby* had a format, as did your papers for history and science. They had a beginning, a middle and an end. You did not just ramble. You focused on a single point and stuck to it, describing and developing your insights and observations. At the end, you returned to your main idea, summarized and refocused.

A paragraph on the economic causes of the Civil War might have looked like this:

Beginning:	Some of the causes of the Civil War were economic
Middle:	A sentence or two on Northern prosperity
	A sentence or two on Southern agricultural economy
	Three or four sentences on the conflicts these different economies created in trade, standard of living, and relations with England
End:	A concluding sentence

Another paper on *The Great Gatsby* might have looked like this:

Beginning:	*The Great Gatsby* explores different kinds of love
Middle:	A paragraph about friendship
	Daisy and Jordan
	Gatsby and Nick
	A paragraph about false love
	Nick and Jordan
	Myrtle and Tom
	A paragraph about true love
	Gatsby and Daisy
End:	Summary/conclusion

A science paper might have followed this plan:

Main idea:	Desert animals show a significant adaptation to their environment
Body:	A paragraph about adjustment to heat/cold:
	burrowing animals
	cold-blooded animals
	A paragraph about adjustment to weather:
	natural protections from sandstorms
	natural protections from dehydration
	A paragraph about adjustment to limited food:
	storing nourishment
	extracting water
Conclusion:	A summary or conclusion drawn from the above

The structure of formal writing has been described in this way:

Tell 'em what you're gonna tell 'em

Tell 'em

Tell 'em what you told 'em

This is a good way to think of your writing. The three parts are a natural way to present any topic. After all, you are leading the reader along an unfamiliar path. You have to give that reader an idea of the basic subject so she can focus her attention. The middle will be meaningful if she's got a focus to follow; she can keep an eye out for the romantic theme or important economic factors. Likewise, with a reiteration or closing comment at the end, you strengthen the coherence of your argument.

You've used this three-part pattern in a variety of situations.

The paragraph	The essay
Topic sentence	Introduction
Development	Body
End sentence	Conclusion

No matter what your writing background, you have worked with this common structural pattern. It has been part of your school curriculum for a number of years, and it is something you have practiced. It is a skill that seems to come naturally to most writers when they want to explain something or describe an idea unfamiliar to their readers. Even work on the school newspaper or personal writing may have given you practice in this three-part format:

To jmcelroy@gmail.com

From jhendrickson@cox.net

Subject: summer *topic* *evidence*

Hey you ... my summer rocked. I finally got my license! Then in July ... [a trip, a job, the news about Kate, etc.]. It was the best. So what's up with you?

Later, Jen *conclusion*

You have been taught this structure, and it is just what you need for the college essay. (Sample 1 in Chapter 8 is a good example.) It is also the underlying structure of a lot of college writing, business writing, journal articles, proposals, reports, and speeches. If you're a bit shaky about how it works, pay careful attention to Chapter 3, "Writing an Essay," because you'll need this skill now and later.

The Style

You're experienced with the structure you'll need for the essay, and there's more good news. You have also had 12 years of writing practice. You know the difference between academic and personal writing, between term papers and diaries, between essays and love letters.

Everyone has a natural storehouse of different styles of speech and of writing. You talk to the person taking your order at the local pizza joint with a different vocabulary and style than you use when asked "License and registration?" So you automatically write for each assignment in a different way. Without being conscious of it, you use a style and vocabulary for a paper on *Hamlet* that is nothing like what you'd use in writing an SMS to your best friend. You know when you have to check your spelling and you automatically strive for the level of vocabulary and correctness suitable for each piece of work.

> In his tragic play *Hamlet, Prince of Denmark*, Shakespeare presents a character who's like totally freaked by his father's death.

Whoops! The humor here is a result of mismatched styles.

Most writers move back and forth between various levels of language and styles of writing as easily as they adapt their speech to their listeners. You know the right level of language for a given situation and you know the college essay is a serious piece of writing. But it is not as formal as most school writing; you'll want all the clarity and correctness you can produce but, considering the subject (you), you'll also want a more direct and personal tone than you might otherwise use. In fact, a conversational tone is best. Susan Paton, college counselor at the Hopkins School in Connecticut, says, "We encourage students to use their natural voice and forget the ten-dollar words." Spelling and sentence structure should be correct, but your word choice and style should not be heavily academic, full of thesaurus words, or unnatural.

You have a good idea of what your strengths and weaknesses are as a writer. (For a fresh look, browse through your writing folder from last semester, or ask your English teacher.) You have plenty of time to proofread, look up potential problem words, and edit your essay. Any flow of good ideas can be interrupted by dum errers; save time to proofread thoroughly and correct your own dumb errors.

You certainly have adequate motivation built into this situation. It's only a matter of diligence to bring your performance to perfection and, again, you've had 12 years of practice.

The Subject

The greatest strength you bring to this essay is 17+ years of familiarity with the topic: YOU. The form and style are familiar, and best of all, you are the world-class expert on this subject.

You know a lot about you. If you can write about wars, novels, experiments, and sonnets, writing about yourself should be simple. You don't have to do any research. You don't have to study the major city-states of the Renaissance or read *Macbeth*. You already know all you need to know. And there is a wealth of information, thousands of incidents, events, and facts from which to draw. Instead of being at a loss for material, you may find the quantity a little overwhelming. However, you don't have to despair of finding a topic; it has been the subject of your close scrutiny every morning since you were tall enough to look into the bathroom mirror.

Another wonderful aspect of this topic is that no one else has it; it is unique. No essay will directly compete with yours. You've picked colleges that are appropriate for you, probably a group of similar schools that include a "long shot" and a "likely." They are tailored to you and you are, therefore, tailored to them. Your desires, plans, and abilities probably fall within a profile of each college's student body, so your essay has every reason to stand up to the other submissions.

Remember, the colleges are not looking for a single answer. Admission personnel do not look for a specific student. Occidental College's application advises: "Be yourself — don't feel obligated to write what you think would impress us. We appreciate honesty, clarity and passion!" Thus, there is no set combination of items that every applicant must have in order to gain acceptance at a certain college. You, your essay, and your application profile do not have to match a single narrow standard. They need only fit into one of the constituencies, into the larger pattern of students at your chosen school.

The best part of the college essay is that it can't be wrong. One of my students wrote an entire paper on "The Love Song of J. Alfred Prufrock" as a poem set in an aquarium. It turned out she had read the line about the yellow fog and thought it was "the yellow frog" that pressed its nose against the windowpane! But had she said she loved aquariums, who could possibly question that? Everyone laughed at the boy who thought "On First Looking into Chapman's Homer" was about baseball, but an essay on an imagined lunch with Babe Ruth would be a different story. Follow the advice of Amy Abrams, dean of admission and financial aid at Sarah Lawrence College: "Take a deep breath, relax and believe in yourself." There is no fixed critical opinion about you, no standard theory of interpretation. You can't come off looking bad because you didn't know that Richard Wright was a Communist, that Hamlet's problem was melancholia, that "Stopping by Woods on a Snowy Evening" might be about suicide. You don't have to do research. You have had lots of experience with this "text" and you are the major authority in the field.

The topic may seem hard, but it's really the essay's greatest attraction. It's about you — a topic you know, need to know, want to talk about, have as your exclusive territory, and can't be wrong about. You are the expert and can easily speak with both authority and conviction.

The Process

Finally, the process of all school papers is the process you will use for the application essay. You will want to brainstorm a little, organize a lot, write, rewrite and edit. Chapter 3 is a guide to the composition process. But the thought process is the same as well: focus and prove.

Let's look back at that first paper on *The Great Gatsby*. You were assigned a topic: hope. You explored the novel and drew out the incidents that proved Fitzgerald portrayed different kinds of hope (like Nick's move to the East Coast in search of success on Wall Street). You gathered as many examples as made your point vivid and then described them to the extent that they supported your theme.

The application of this process to the college essay is simple. In this case, you look into your life, select an aspect of yourself that you see as a strength, a personal characteristic like commitment or creativity or resilience, one that may not come through in the rest of your application's facts, grades, and numbers. Then you find the substantiating evidence — an event, experience, or incident — that reveals this aspect. Determination? How about four years riding the bench for junior varsity soccer. Insight? Maybe that growing understanding that friends who say, "I'll save you a seat" and then forget to save you a seat aren't really friends. You are the starting point. Events are the evidence. That fateful summer, that wonderful biology class, that job at the pizza place isn't the focus. Each one is valuable, however, as a lens into your thought process, your way of doing things, your choices and values.

Thus the standard school essay is good preparation for writing a college essay. Academic topics aren't so far from college essay topics. Both are based on the isolation of a single aspect of some dense and complex phenomenon. A war, a novel, a food chain may be good for a day's lesson. But these are too much for an essay topic, and so are you. No teacher has asked you to write on a topic like, "Tell me everything you know about Napoleon." The college doesn't want to hear all about you either. Avoid a shotgun approach; telling everything about yourself is not the idea. Select one thing about yourself and illuminate that. The light from one interesting point will reflect your personality. Less is more here. A small and interesting facet will shine most brightly.

The idea is not so much to be different or noble or scholarly. Scott White, at Morristown High School, says, "You don't have to write like Hemingway." But do try to be vivid and clear. What you want to show is your intensity, enthusiasm, insight, and understanding. This is, after all, what the college wants to see. It's what they hope to measure in the essay and what you'll need to succeed when you're accepted.

Don't panic. You have all the skills you need and the assignment is your best and favorite topic. Your school essays have been your training ground for structure and process. The next chapter will take you step-by-step through that process, useful for writing any essay. Chapters 4 and 5 offer sample college essay questions and some strategies for making the most of this special essay.

However you approach it, keep in mind that your essay is your own exciting opportunity to introduce yourself to a college.

Toolbox: A Timeline for Application Essays

Junior Year

During the School Year

- Listen to the seniors complain about the essays ... but not too much. You'll have everything you need when the time comes.

- Commit yourself to doing well on the writing assignments given in your history and English classes. These skills will help you with application essays and with future college writing. Save a few of the best. "Testing optional" schools may ask for a school essay, with the teacher comments and the grade, as a writing sample.

- Consider keeping a journal or an "idea bank" of thoughts, reflections, and important conversations from which you can later draw inspiration. Definitely keep some sort of diary if you go on a college visitation trip, since many schools ask "Why in particular do you wish to attend X?" Comprehensive notes will provide the necessary details for your answers.

- Ask your English teacher if you can write a personal essay for a class assignment (writing practice is a good thing, and your English teacher knows a lot about writing).

- Draft several possible answers to the Common Application essay prompts (after you've read Chapters 4 and 5). Don't commit to a final decision of topic but stockpile options. "Begun is half done."

Over the Summer

- Look at the questions on sample applications and on the Common Application. Think about more possible answers.

- Talk to your parents. Ask them what they consider to be your strengths and talents.

- Make a list of factors, abilities, and characteristics that would recommend you for inclusion in any group. Think about which of these will already be apparent from your application. Your essay can deepen the reader's understanding of a strength or show a side of you not evident elsewhere in the application; it shouldn't duplicate information found elsewhere. (Example: You may have a long history of involvement with tennis, but your win-loss record and ranking will be in your application. If you want to write about tennis, your essay should be about determination or resilience or adaptability ["My Annoying Doubles Partner"] rather than factual information found in the activities grid.)

Senior Year

Two Months Before Your Deadlines

- Float some ideas past your teachers and school counselors and ask for their reactions.

- Continue to ask yourself questions about your interests and abilities. Choose events or information that reflect those features of your personality. Don't write about something you thought about for the first time an hour ago. Don't try to write about something "no one has ever written about before."

- Focus on what you've thought, not what you've done or where you've been.

- If you are applying Early Decision or Early Action, start writing. The deadline is November 1 for many schools.

One Month Before Your Deadlines

- Write an essay.

- Now write another one (throw the first one away if you tried to squeeze yourself into some sort of story that you think admission wants to hear).

- Put it all away for a few days; think about what you've written and then revise. Consider crossing out the first paragraph of your essay for a faster, more focused beginning.

- Ask for intervention or guidance from a teacher, parent, or counselor well before you consider yourself to be "done." It's hard to accept criticism or advice if you believe you're finished.

- PROOFREAD.

- Resist the temptation to "shop" your essay around for multiple approvals; your final draft needs to sound like you (even if that means you go back and submit your first draft!).

- Keep copies of your essays after you upload them onto the applications.

- PROOFREAD.

- If you apply Early Decision or Early Action and end up making additional applications at the end of December, take a second look at the essay you created in October and be sure it's the best you can do. The Common Application allows two revisions.

- READ YOUR ESSAY ALOUD to find missing words and errors caused by editing.

- When you hit Submit, you can relax. You've done the choosing and you've crafted solid responses. With Lorene Cary, in her memoir *Black Ice*, say, "I wrote as prettily as I could and dared them not to like it." Now the choosing is up the "them."

chapter 3

Writing An Essay

The purpose of this chapter is to review the process of writing any essay. You may be experienced enough with this form to skim this chapter quickly and go right on to Chapters 4 and 5, which apply the general form to the application essay. Check the summary section at the end of this chapter. If the concepts there seem unfamiliar, or if writing has not been your strength in high school, you will want to read and study this chapter carefully before writing the essays for your applications and again when you begin writing essays in college.

What Exactly Is an Essay?

Essays are as diverse as writers themselves and do not conform to as specific a pattern as sonnets or tragedies or lab reports. However, most essays are some sort of a defense of a writer's opinion or point of view. The opinions vary greatly: Shakespeare's plays all deal with the restoration of order; Springfield ought to build a youth activity center; the United States should no longer invest its tax monies in manned space exploration; gerbils need a stable social environment to flourish.

Personal and particular or academic and abstract, the essay tries to convince the reader that an opinion, theory, claim, or interpretation is correct. Thus an essay can be a newspaper editorial advocating reduced taxes, a term paper on *The Color Purple* as a classical tragedy, a proposal from an architectural firm for a shopping mall, or a defense of an innocent client in a court of law. The college essay, too, presents a thesis — a view of the applicant — to the college admission board and persuades them of its validity.

Writing any essay is a process. There are stages and steps to follow. The writer who makes multiple drafts and the one who rarely revises both go through a similar process, either on paper or in their heads. But like Abraham Lincoln, who scribbled a few notes on an envelope on his way to Gettysburg, most writers prefer to complete some of the preliminary steps in writing. The process is:

1. Preparation and prewriting
2. A number of drafts (from one to several)
3. Revising and editing

A 45-minute final examination essay in modern European history might involve:

1. Two minutes of preparation
2. Forty minutes on the single draft you will write
3. Three minutes of quick proofreading and revising

The final essay or term paper for the same course would involve:

1. A few days of planning, thinking, and researching in the library and on the Internet
2. Two drafts or more
3. Editing and revising; optional review by another reader — a friend, teacher, or peer tutor at your school's writing center

The examination essay takes less than an hour; the term paper, one to two weeks. However, the three-part process is used in both writing situations.

Prewriting

The goal of prewriting is to develop your claim by:

1. Brainstorming
2. Asking Questions
3. Focusing
4. Organizing
5. Choosing a Structure

Brainstorming

It's time to clean your room. Throw everything that's not nailed down into a heap in the center: books, clothes, CDs, letters, used coffee cups, that paper plate with its little scabs of pizza sauce. Now you have a sense of how much you have to do and exactly with what you have to work. Piles can be sorted from the central mess—one for the laundry, one to be saved, one to go in the trash, and so on. Many writers begin with a similar fast and disorganized collection of potential ideas. They throw every possibility onto a list or into a data file and then look at the result. Patterns, groups, and an overall sense of what they have to work with begin to emerge. This is brainstorming.

Grab a piece of paper or sit down at a computer. Write the limits of your assignment on the top of the page: 750 words on my summer vacation, a paragraph on the importance of the National Labor Relations Act, a three-to five-page paper on Emily Dickinson, a 10-page paper on global warming. Now put down everything you can think of that relates to the topic. List single words that pop into your mind. Ask yourself questions about the topic, make statements, wonder, speculate, recall, and connect. Set a timer or otherwise establish a time limit so that you will keep on writing for several minutes. Do not stop to daydream or reread. Just write, write, write.

Here are two different samples of students' 3-minute brainstorms on *The Simpsons*.

Sample 1

I love The Simpsons — everyone watches it — people say "D'oh!" now like Homer, the American 'Everyman' — they live in a little town, Springfield, but it has everything (nuclear power plant, airport, desert) — they all look yellow — I love the episode about the trillion dollar bill, when Homer has to get it back but Castro steals it — and the ones about who shot Mr. Burns — Homer lives for beer and donuts and television — a typical (is it?) American family, the challenges — I know about 20 episodes by heart — is that normal?

(This student jotted down a stream-of-consciousness response of his personal feelings about the topic.)

Here's another approach:

Sample 2

A cartoon sitcom

Created by Matt Groening; now written by a team

Maggie is perpetually one year old, Lisa is always in the second grade; Bart is in fourth grade

Bart's best friend is Milhouse

Bart likes to prank-call Moe

Mr. Burns owns the nuclear power plant

Homer is always falling asleep at work

The Simpsons' cat is named Snowball 2 — who was Snowball 1?

Most of the shows divide into three sub-episodes

They emphasize family a lot — love but also conflicts (sisters-in-law, Grampa)

Apu runs the convenience store

The Flanders live next door — very religious

Lots of guest appearances — Bob Hope, Mel Gibson, Jay Leno, U2, Lisa Kudrow

Sideshow Bob was Krusty the Clown's sidekick, but now it's Sideshow Mel

They criticize big companies: time shares, Microsoft, NASA, SUVs, the tomacco

Marge has blue hair and older twin sisters

Maggie costs $847.63 in the opening credit

They go to Reverend Lovejoy's church

They often tackle theology — God even appears — and great literature (*Hamlet*, Maya Angelou, Edgar Allan Poe, Amy Tan)

(This student seems knowledgeable about the topic; she produced a more detailed list of thoughts.)

This stream-of-consciousness collecting process doesn't require a keyboard or even paper and pencil. Some writers mull over an idea for days or weeks or even years. But a significant percentage of writers use a journal, diary, or notebook: They write as a way to begin thinking about writing. Nathaniel Hawthorne, for one, kept such a journal:

> *The life of a woman, who, by the old colony law, was condemned always to wear the letter A, sewed on her garment, in token of her having committed adultery.*

The Scarlet Letter, and quite a few other Hawthorne stories, can be traced to the brainstorming he did in this journal. So, for many writing assignments, the way to begin (especially if beginning is difficult and you aren't sure where to begin) is to make lists like those above, brainstorming thoughts and responses to the assignment and seeing exactly with what you have to work.

Asking Questions

At this point, you should feel some positive momentum from discovering that you do, in fact, know something about your subject. This is an ideal time to go over your notes and jottings, ask questions, and look for useful repetitions and/or connectable ideas. You are moving toward a focus. In the second *Simpsons* example, there is a mix of themes and facts about the show. A few of the facts are about the show itself, but most have to do with characters in the Simpsons' immediate family or various supporting characters; almost all relate to other items on the list.

A cartoon sitcom
Created by Matt Groening;
now written by a team
Maggie is perpetually one year old,
Lisa is always in the second grade,
Bart is in third grade
Bart's best friend is Milhouse   Minor Characters
Bart likes to prank-call Moe
The Creative   Mr. Burns owns the nuclear power plant
Process   Homer is always falling asleep at work
The Simpsons' cat is named Snowball 2
—who was Snowball 1?
Most of the shows divide into three sub-episodes

The Creative
Process

Themes

They emphasize family a lot—love but also conflicts
(sisters-in-law)
Apu runs the convenience store
The Flanders live next door—very religious
Lots of guest appearances—Bob Hope,
Mel Gibson, Jay Leno, U2, George Bush
Sideshow Bob was Krusty the Clown's
sidekick, but now it's Sideshow Mel
They criticize big companies: time shares,
Microsoft, NASA, SUV's, the tomacco
Marge has blue hair and older twin sisters
Maggie costs $847.63 in the opening credit
They go to Reverend Lovejoy's church
They often tackle theology—God even appears
—and great literature (*Hamlet*, Maya Angelou,
Edgar Allan Poe, Amy Tan)

Minor
Characters

Minor
Characters

Any one of these could lead to a topic and then to a thesis for an essay.

You can now increase your power over your ideas by going over your notes several times, adding any new thoughts that come to you. Enjoy unearthing the ways your ideas are coming together; look for themes or patterns among the items you've listed. Most important, ask yourself key questions like these:

- Why do the characters never grow older?

- Is family presented as a good thing or a source of conflict?

- Why is *The Simpsons* so popular?

- What makes *The Simpsons* so funny ... to adults and to kids?

- Is Homer Simpson a brief fad or a more important comment on culture?

- Do girls like *The Simpsons* as much as boys?

- Is Marge the voice of reason?

- Are women presented more positively than men?

- Can a cartoon be both humorous *and* serious?

- What are the connecting ideas that run through the series?

What you are doing now is analyzing your topic, breaking it down into pieces by asking the what, how, and why questions. *The Simpsons* is too big a topic for an essay; let's see how concentrating on one element of its popularity, its humor, or its production helps you create a stronger essay. This principle is familiar from your school assignments, as well; an essay for English might focus on one element of a poem: form, language, setting, tone, theme. A history essay on a president might focus on one campaign strategy, one conflict with Congress, one area of policy. A college application essay works best when it focuses on one aspect of your personality. Getting at a worthwhile aspect begins with questions:

- Why is this important? How can I show readers its impact?
- What is the purpose or function of this one element?
- Why did this occur?
- What was the impact of this one event, decision, scene, choice?
- What evidence can I give of the further importance or impact of this?

Focusing

You're good to go now. Your essay will explore and support a single claim or thesis. If this is a 45-minute midterm, latch onto the first topic that jumps off the page and get to the writing as quickly as possible. If this is an out-of-class essay, you will shift and adjust your thesis as you work on other parts of your essay, but one angle or aspect of a large and complex topic is your beginning.

Let's now look at the groups and clusters of ideas you have come up with and try making statements about some of them.

- *The Simpsons* is successful because it appeals to both adults and kids.
- *The Simpsons* explores complicated issues such as materialism, God, death, prejudice, and morality.
- The Simpsons as a family are endearing because of their faults.

These are preliminary thesis statements and any one of them is a good start: each focuses on an aspect of *The Simpsons* and asserts an opinion or claim about the show.

One interesting sentence can be the basis of a persuasive argument. From the groups of ideas from your brainstorming and the questions you've asked yourself, make a list of possible thesis statements. If time allows, consult with your teacher or professor about these possible topics. If a full-length research paper is the assignment, seek out ideas on the Internet and then use the library's resources — from books and periodicals to databases in your field of interest. Librarians know a lot, too. Any one of these might supplement the brainstorming process and help you narrow down and select a topic. You are now ready to choose the topic that most interests you, the topic about which you have the most to say, the most specific topic you can devise; then get on to the business of making a simple plan.

Organizing

You have chosen a focus; you have a tentative thesis statement. You probably are not ready to create a final outline, but it is wise to impose a little order at this point. As a next step, let's see how you can go about proving your claim.

Revise your brainstorm results and eliminate ideas unrelated to your topic. It may be painful to cross items out, but you can't include everything. A paper that tries to include *everything* is not an essay; it's still just a brainstorm. Some students write to present everything they know and hope the teacher will hunt through the forest of ideas for what he or she "wants to see." This strategy makes the reader work too hard to see which ideas are valuable. Better to prove a small point than require the reader to find the meaning in a jumble of information. The point here? When you cut away the excess, your best ideas will be easy to find. Fire up the delete key and start cutting.

To produce the best work, if time and the assignment dictate, you will want to research your topic further. Reread the primary material, consult critical sources, talk again with your teacher. Add more evidence to support your proposed thesis statement. Once you are satisfied that you have solid, supporting information, rearrange your brainstorm sheet into a tentative list of points or supporting ideas for your topic. To help you see how this works, here are three samples of early organizational efforts that include a preliminary thesis and a general plan of proof to be covered in the essay:

THESIS: Shakespeare's plays often deal with the restoration of order.

1. *Romeo and Juliet:* The conflict between the Capulets and the Montagues must give way to peace and order.

2. *The Taming of the Shrew:* Kate's aggressive attempts to dominate men must yield to a more orderly and peaceful relationship between men and women.

3. *Hamlet:* Hamlet's burden is the ghost's command that he restore order by avenging his father's murder.

THESIS: Gerbils need a stable social environment to flourish.

1. The control group
   a. eating habits
   b. growth
   c. behavior
   d. mating habits

2. The experimental group
   a. eating habits
   b. growth
   c. behavior
   d. mating habits

THESIS: *The Simpsons* is a serious cartoon.

Adult world of work/life in suburbia

Money and business themes

Good and evil — serious issues

The world the way children see it

Choosing a Structure

As you create a simple outline, choose an appropriate order for your points. How might you decide what is the most persuasive order of ideas? One common organizational plan is by time. Discuss a process step-by-step, the events in a novel in the order in which they happened, the plays of Shakespeare in the order in which they were written. Or consider what your readers already know and what they might want to learn. Often, the most useful order of points in an essay is from least to most important. Remember that the goal of an essay is to persuade. It is therefore logical to begin with the small and familiar and build toward the unfamiliarity and complexity of your argument. When you borrow money from your parents, you mention how responsible you've been recently, your good grades last semester, and other facts that set the stage. But your big persuasions — your safe driving record, your plan to fill the car with gas, how desperately you need it — come at the end. You don't start big and fade; you tuck in any less powerful points early on and save up for the grand finale.

The same principle applies to writing. The writer of the essay on *The Simpsons* looks over the four ideas: Springfield, money, good/evil, and family. She continues to ask questions: What do I mean by serious? Serious to whom? Can a cartoon be serious? What are cartoons, anyway — are they the same as other art, but just graphically different? What makes *The Simpsons* serious? Whose world is this? She refines her claim or thesis and then revises her ideas, regroups, and builds her argument toward the most persuasive point. The final plan might look something like this:

THESIS: *The Simpsons* seems like an adult cartoon, but it is really a child's world that's depicted.

1. *The Simpsons* has many elements of serious, adult entertainment.
   a. The universal suburban town: Springfield (there are Springfields in New Jersey, Massachusetts, Illinois, etc.).
   b. Life in the suburbs: house on a street, the mall, driving everywhere, school, local bar.
   c. Themes of family life: the kids (gambling the Christmas money), Grampa, sisters-in-law.
   d. Money and business: Mr. Burns as embodiment of capitalistic excess, no one ever pays the tab at Moe's, Apu's entrepreneurial dreams, Homer's crazy schemes (selling grease; the tomacco).
   e. Social criticism: violence on TV ("Itchy and Scratchy"), corporate corruption, public versus private schools.

2. But the show appeals to children because it's an ideal child's world.
   a. Springfield seems to be the whole world: dam, airport, Civil War cemetery — an all-purpose town.
   b. Family is focused mostly on the children (Lisa's school choice, Bart's homework).
   c. Work unrealistically portrayed as pointless or corrupt: Homer sleeps or schemes, Burns exploits workers.
   d. Adults are unreliable, out of touch with reality, likely to make mistakes (Principal Skinner, Ned Flanders, Moe).

    e. Everything bad is temporary — crashed cars, broken arms, the house demolished in a town's revenge — and calamities are cured or corrected in the next episode.

    f. Children are wise (Lisa — college applications, solving the mystery, saving the day) or at least wiseguys (Bart).

Conclusion: No one ever ages on *The Simpsons* because it is meant to be a world ruled by children.

Since the first section of this essay offers an interpretation that is rejected by the second section, the organization is established by the thesis: what you might think, followed by what you should think.

This organizing process is not a substitute for the final outline you need for a 15-page research paper, but it is an adequate preparation for most short essays or essay test answers and a necessary first step if such a final outline is required. For longer essays, a well-designed outline keeps you in harness with your ideas and in sync with your readers.

Summary: Getting the Most Out of Prewriting

The prewriting process can take you from the bewilderment of having just received an assignment to confidence in being ready to write. Use it as much as you need. You may brainstorm and organize a test answer in a total of five minutes, or mull over ideas for weeks, brainstorming three or four times, and then sitting down to compose a final outline. Most writers need some help and preparation; they gather their ideas together in a brainstorm, sort and group them, ask questions about their first thoughts, focus on a tentative thesis, and then organize their proof in a logical pattern.

Drafting

Now complete the research and rereading of sources; continue to ask questions, refine and regroup your ideas. Then begin to write your essay in these three parts: introduction, body, conclusion. Although the three parts work together, they need to be thought of separately. The introduction and conclusion are necessary frames for the real substance of your essay, the body. Like the bread in a sandwich, the introduction and conclusion keep everything neat, organized, and together. In between lies the important business, the evidence or proof itself. All three parts make the whole.

The Introduction

There are essentially two strategies for an introduction. One is to provide the reader with a road map for the area about to be covered. This is especially helpful if the territory is tricky or the journey is long, as with a complex or extensive essay. The underlying principle is to provide the reader with a sort of outline of the essay's content.

The Road Map Introduction

Thesis (main idea)

Reference to each major point of the essay

A concluding sentence that returns, in different words, to the thesis

Here is an example of this type of introduction for an essay on the novels of Charles Dickens:

Dickens's novels often present children as the adults or "parents" in their families. In early works like *Nicholas Nickleby*, the real parents are basically unreliable. The children cannot count on them for support, guidance, or love. But the problem intensifies in works like *Bleak House* where adults often act like children. In Dickens's last completed novel, *Our Mutual Friend*, Jenny Wren and Lizzie Hexam suggest the final extension of this theme: they are mothers to their own fathers. Throughout Dickens's works it is the children who run things and hold the families together, while the adults fantasize, dream, or drink.

This introduction does not actually discuss the examples or prove the point of the essay, but it leaves no doubt as to what will be discussed and in what order. It names the thesis, outlines three supporting points that will be treated (*Nicholas Nickleby*, *Bleak House*, and *Our Mutual Friend*), and allows the reader to see the general plan of the whole essay. This type of introduction is most common in scientific and social science writing and provides the reader with an "abstract" of the essay.

The General-to-Specific Introduction

Here is another kind of introduction; this one does not outline the paper. Instead, it draws the reader into the topic slowly, leaving the presentation of individual points to the body of the essay:

> A general statement (in the topic area)
>
> More specific statements that lead to the thesis
>
> Thesis (main idea or claim)

As a helpful comparison, let's now look at an example of this type of introduction for the same paper on the novels of Dickens.

The 19th century took the family seriously. Queen Victoria and Prince Albert were a model family, the parents of nine children. And in the novels that were meant to be read to the family group, family connections and relationships were major themes. Charles Dickens's novels explore these themes and, as the unhappily married father of 10 children, he knew what family life was like. His novels, however, often present the family in a rather inverted way.

This introduction slowly defines the areas to be discussed and gradually brings the reader to the topic. The sample begins with the 19th century and 19th-century families, then goes on to Dickens's own family, and finally to the families in Dickens's novels. The actual novels are not named, but the topic is pointed at (but not actually stated) in the last sentence.

This type of introduction is remarkably flexible. It can be brief or lengthy. The opening can be many things; here, background information — a few words about the author and the time period — begins the essay. A definition could also have been used. Select the right introduction by thinking about what your reader already knows and what they need to learn from you. A science paper on eating habits might want to define "eating" in a broader sense than usual in order to discuss ingestive behaviors in one-celled organisms. For a paper on unemployment for a broad, nonexpert audience, the introduction could begin with a common assumption and then contradict it:

> Jobs are scarce. Unemployment is up and people are holding on to whatever jobs they have. There's not much movement in major corporations and, when people retire or depart, their work is absorbed by the survivors. Yet this may be the best time in the last 10 years to look for a new job.

Editorials, blogs, and magazine articles often use this introduction strategy, capturing the reader's attention with a brief story or incident:

> The hot night of July 26, 2012, threatened a thunderstorm in Henderson, Texas. When Nancy-Jean Alberts went out to empty the trash, she noticed the sky was dark for 7 p.m. and lines of heat lightning darted along the horizon.

This article might turn out to be about a murder, a flood, or even trash. The narration at the beginning catches the readers' attention and draws them into the paragraph; a forceful and focused thesis statement will follow.

The general-to-specific introduction is flexible and simple. You have some choices in its construction and do not have to give away all your ideas in the first paragraph. It is suitable for most essays and is especially useful for those in a timed situation when you may not know at the beginning exactly what points (or how many) you will cover. One important reminder about the first sentence — you want to interest your reader. So don't be overly general. "Life is interesting" doesn't sound very interesting and would require a very lengthy paragraph to narrow it down adequately to a thesis. "Shakespeare is a great playwright" is certainly more specific, but it lacks impact. "Shakespeare is my new BFF" is memorable … but not in a good way. You're inviting your reader to care about your thoughts. Make your tone an invitation to read on. Write a first sentence that is interesting and related to the thesis but engage the reader's interest without being confusing, silly, or shocking.

Is an Introduction Absolutely Necessary?

Most essays need a paragraph of some length to identify the topic and get things going, but there are a few exceptions. A short essay (one or two paragraphs) does not need an introduction. A few sentences at the beginning of the first paragraph can make the topic clear. Some tests and examinations (and most college application essays) provide only a few minutes or a suggested word limit for your responses. In such a case, a full introduction would waste precious time and space. If you are given an essay test with several questions, a good first sentence might serve as the introduction to the shorter answers. If you'll receive only 15 points for an answer to "How did Metternich influence diplomacy in the 19th century?" begin with a sentence drawn from the question itself (you might simply state that Metternich did change diplomatic techniques), and give the rest of the allotted time and space to the proof of your claim. If your application essay must present "you" in 650 words, don't give more than 50 words to getting under way.

Another time to consider omitting the introduction is in an inductive essay. This essay takes the reader through a discussion without fully revealing the focus, unwrapping the direction only at the end. This is a suspenseful and creative approach to the essay and can be very effective. But, it is best reserved for less stressful situations than the college essay, for the most able writers, and for short, creative topics.

Finally, a *narrative* essay might survive without an introduction. The writer tells a story, recounts a series of incidents, and then draws meaning from them in the conclusion. Like the inductive essay, this format requires readers to go some distance on faith. They aren't sure to what they ought to be paying attention, but finally it all makes sense in the conclusion. This strategy can make a very effective short college essay, but since it puts a significant burden on the reader, it is best reserved for occasional use by highly skilled writers.

Most of the time, you'll want an introduction that invites the reader to think through your ideas with you. Either the road map introduction or the general-to-specific format can provide that strong start and clear direction.

The Body

The substance of your essay is the body. Bound in place by the introduction and the conclusion, the body does the work of the essay: It proves. It presents the evidence that will convert the reader to your opinion. Each paragraph of the body is a block of proof, a chunk of evidence of the validity for your claim, and each is developed from one aspect or point of your thesis, as sketched out in the simple outline.

The Shakespeare essay, for example, uses three plays as examples to prove that Shakespeare was concerned with the restoration of order. The outline gives three subtopics: order in *Romeo and Juliet*, in *The Taming of the Shrew*, and in *Hamlet*. Thus, you plan three paragraphs for the body, one for each play. If, however, in drafting the essay you discover new aspects of the topic that should be mentioned — perhaps that *Hamlet* is a play about both the proper order in a kingdom and also about one man's drive for proper family order through the revenge of his father's murder — the plan can be expanded and the number of paragraphs in the body adjusted, in this case, to four, one for each play and two for *Hamlet*.

The important thing is to prove, with specific and vivid detail, the correctness of your claim. To persuade your reader, you must present a sequence of arguments for your thesis rather than plot summaries, story outlines, or a review of the course of history thus far.

Selection is the key. Go through each part of your argument and select the scenes, details, quotations, and facts that show the truth of your view. To substantiate your thesis, bring the reader's attention to the evidence that cumulatively shows that you are correct. Select. Do not retell! It is not persuasive to retell a novel, review every event of a war, or summarize everything that has been said on your topic. Your essay should be based on your angle of vision, your special lens, your way of looking at a larger complex of ideas. And in support of your thesis, you need to gather only those points or ideas that prove your view is right.

Each paragraph of the body should conform to this pattern (or vary from it for a good reason):

Topic Sentence
(the main idea of this paragraph and its relation to the thesis)

Development
(the evidence — events, facts, statistics, reasons, examples, details, things said in the literature, things said about the literature — presented in some logical order)

End Sentence
(especially useful in a long or complex paragraph)

Topic Sentence

The topic sentence is important in two ways: It identifies the subject of the paragraph, and it shows how the paragraph is connected to the thesis. It may even form a transition from the previous paragraph.

1. thesis — Shakespeare explored the instability of life and the
2. transition — need for order not only in a comic setting but also
3. topic — in the tragic circumstances of Prince Hamlet.

1. topic — But things get worse in *Our Mutual Friend*.
2. transition — Now parents and adults are not just silly and
3. thesis — irresponsible; they are the children of the families.

In the first example, the writer reiterates, in slightly different words, the main thesis of the essay, mentions the point of the previous paragraph (a comedy's treatment of this theme), and then establishes what this paragraph will discuss (*Hamlet*). In the second instance, the writer uses two sentences to get going: the first names the paragraph's topic (*Our Mutual Friend*) whereas the second fits that topic into the larger scheme of the thesis (irresponsibility and childish adults).

There is, and always should be, flexibility in a format. Every paragraph does not have to begin with a reference to the preceding paragraph. A topic sentence doesn't have to be first in a paragraph, either. But each sentence that appears before the topic sentence runs the risk of being wasted. Your readers don't yet know what's going on and may lose interest or the sense of continuity. They ask, "Why am I reading this?" Therefore, it is helpful if each paragraph declares — and usually the sooner the better — its topic and how it intends to support the essay's claim.

Development

The middle of each paragraph is the support, the meat in the sandwich. It is a combination of facts, events, quotations, examples, and reasons that proves the point of that paragraph and, in so doing, proves the thesis of the essay. It is the evidence that will persuade your reader. Notice the combination of different types of support in this paragraph from an essay about insanity in *Moby Dick*.

Another way Melville makes the reader aware of the transition from sanity to insanity is in his imagery. Throughout the novel, he weaves a careful pattern of images that turn from normal to abnormal, from familiar to strange. For example, the images of fire begin in the friendly inns of Nantucket and New Bedford. Ishmael rejoices in the privilege of "making my own summer with my own coals" (61). Fire is here warmth and companionship. Even Queequeg's sacrificial fire to Yojo serves as the beginning of intimate friendship between the two sailors. But slowly this begins to change. By the middle of the novel, fire begins to suggest evil. It is associated with Ahab's mad purpose, what critic Richard Chase in *The American Novel and Its Tradition* calls "the self-absorption that leads to isolation, madness and suicide" (109). Ahab calls himself a volcano in "The Quarter-Deck" chapter and the crew swears death to Moby Dick in a fiery crossing of harpoons. Later, in the chapter called "The Tryworks," Ishmael compares the rendering fires to the fires of hell. By Chapter 113, hot-forged harpoons are being dipped in blood as Ahab baptizes the crew "*in nomine diabolis*" (373). Nature's fire, lightning, warns the crew away by igniting the masts and nearly striking Ahab. The happy homefires of Nantucket have changed into the dangerous fires of Ahab's mad passion; thus they reinforce the novel's movement from sanity to insanity.

Like Melville's imagery, his characters, too, move toward madness. First there is Pip . . . .

Right margin annotations:
Example
Quotation
Event
Critic's Opinion
Event
Detail
Event
Quotation
Events

End Sentence

At the end of a paragraph, a sentence that summarizes the whole paragraph and refocuses on the essay's thesis can strengthen the essay's coherence. Because this sentence echoes the topic sentence, you may wonder if the paper isn't getting repetitious. "Isn't it awfully boring to say this one thing at the beginning and end of the paper, and at the beginning and end of every paragraph, too?" But you are covering ideas familiar and clear only to you; your readers (ideally) have never thought exactly this way about this topic.

They have to be led a little so there has to be repetition. Each topic sentence should sound somewhat alike. Each should relate to the thesis. The concluding sentences of some, or all, of the body paragraphs will return to the main idea of the essay, too. There will be changes in wording and perhaps only the repetition of a key word (such as "order" in the Shakespeare essay) to remind readers of what's happening. But signs and repetitions along the way keep readers on your path. The end of the paragraph about *Moby Dick* is a good example of this kind of helpful repetition.

A short or simple paragraph, or one that appears right before the conclusion, does not need the summary sentence at the end. You can draw the paragraph to a close in some other way, perhaps simply by adding a sentence that makes it clear the paragraph is complete.

Remember to follow a logical order in the presentation of the body's paragraphs. Chronological order or order of location may suit your topic. And order of importance, beginning with minor points and building toward the most important argument at the end, is always a good choice.

The body of the essay is its most important part. You marshal all the evidence you can find to support your theory and present it in a series of paragraphs designed to convince your readers. Most of these paragraphs will begin with a topic sentence that connects the paragraph to the thesis. All of them will be made up of facts, examples, and extensive specific support for your claim. Many will end with a summarizing clincher that redirects the reader's attention to the thesis. The repetitions of the thesis and its rewording in topic sentences and end sentences are useful reiterations; they provide the necessary coherence that creates the focus. The body should be by far the greatest percentage of the essay for it is there that the essay will win its argument.

The Conclusion

The conclusion can serve one or two functions. It should refocus the readers' attention on the main idea of the essay, remind them of what they have just read, and reaffirm the validity of the author's argument. This is the summary conclusion and, although not particularly creative, it gets the job done. The format is:

> Thesis (slightly reworded)
>
> Reference to the major points of the body (in order)
>
> End sentence

A more creative use of the conclusion is as a springboard for a new idea. After refocusing and briefly summarizing, the writer goes on to judge, speculate, generalize, or recommend.

Thesis (slightly reworded)

Short summary of the essay

Additional idea that grows logically from what has been proven in the essay

This type of conclusion does not suit every topic, as there will be times when you do not have anything to add to the end of your essay. Yet, take note of this opportunity as there are many times when it can work for you. Here are four examples:

1. The essay on Shakespeare's theme of order might end with a generalization about Elizabethan England, the order people saw in their world, and political anxiety about the Tudor succession. You would thus connect this particular theme from three of Shakespeare's plays to larger trends and ideas of his age.

2. An essay on the athletic facilities at your school, in which you urge the creation of an all-weather track, might recommend the creation of a capital fund campaign to raise the money needed for the project. The essay itself would only show the need and value of the track. Having reiterated those ideas in the conclusion, you could go on to suggest how the work might get done.

3. An essay on a gerbil experiment might speculate on other possible parallel experiments that could be performed.

4. A college essay describing an applicant might use the conclusion to connect goals and personal qualities to the college itself. For example, if you have proven you are a physics geek, in your conclusion you might show why MIT is the logical choice for you.

To determine whether this type of conclusion is appropriate, at the end of your essay ask yourself, "So what? What does all that I've proven mean? Where can I go from here?" If there isn't any real answer to this, then sum up and stop. If a suggestion or generalization comes to mind, you might use it for a springboard conclusion.

This conclusion is especially useful for assigned essay topics that request the writer to discuss two unequal ideas. For example, a history teacher might ask: "To what extent did the role of women in society change during the 1930s? Do you see any parallels in the situation of women today?" The real heart of this question is the role of women in the 1930s. An additional, although less important, part of the question asks the student to assess his or her life in terms of what's been said about the 1930s. The student constructs an essay with individual paragraphs devoted to areas of change concerning women: the domestic scene, the job market, economic power, fashion. The conclusion might sum up these points and then go on to comment on the writer's own time. Since this is a lesser part of the question, it could be adequately treated as the final aspect of a conclusion. Judgments and comparisons could be based on what has already been said in the body.

This second type of conclusion would not be a good choice if the question asked for the discussion of two equal points: "Discuss the forces that created the League of Nations and those that destroyed it." Here, the best bet is a body divided into two sections, one on creation and one on destruction. The conclusion would then merely summarize what was presented in the body.

Summary: Getting the Most Out of Drafting

As you plan and write the essay, how much you say, the importance of the various parts of the essay, the structure of the paragraphs themselves, and the repetition needed will emerge. Think of your readers and choose an introduction that will engage and guide them; create body paragraphs in support of your thesis; select an appropriate conclusion.

Patterns are useful. Good tailors begin with standard patterns and soon develop their own. So it is with writers. The idea is to begin with rules and use them where appropriate. There is no reason why you can't "break" a rule as long as you have a reason and are doing so consciously. The goal of any writing advice is to help writers be more aware and in control of their material and to avoid writing with no idea why they are at one point succeeding and at another failing. "You didn't like my paper" is one student comment that drives me crazy. I've never graded a paper on whether I liked it or not. The paper grades itself — according to how successfully the writer organizes the material and validates the claims.

Also, keep in mind that there is no secret set of "right" answers stashed in the school safe. The purpose of an essay is not to guess what the teacher believes about a topic and win an A; it is to develop a good thesis and prove it. Critical opinion changes, even among the leaders in a given field. Notice the ups and downs that the reputations of presidents suffer. Consider the esteem with which Freud was regarded in the 1950s versus the respect awarded him in the feminist age. To paraphrase Emerson, "Ask for no man's opinion but your own." Every age must write its own criticism. So the essay is not about latching onto THE ONE RIGHT ANSWER. It is about your ability to find a possible answer and to make a convincing argument for it.

An interesting idea with no evidence is a pointless exercise; a lot of plot review or a collection of facts without a focus can read as wandering exposition. Think of two opposing lawyers; each has the same events and facts to work with yet the prosecutor selects and presents them so the accused looks like a cold-blooded murderer while the attorney for the defense selects and presents them so that the client seems as innocent as an angel. Every winning argument needs a good claim and a focused selection of supporting material to make it clear and convincing.

This is especially true for the college essay. Many students set out to "tell them what they want to hear." This is a fruitless and contradictory goal. What the essay should provide is a sense of you, a concrete and specific view with the facts to back it up.

It's a straight and narrow path with temptations on every side: the risk-taker's razzle-dazzle idea with no evidence, the "everything but the kitchen sink" essay, full of facts and plot review, with no focus. In any essay (and especially in the college essay), you need both focus and evidence.

A Special Organizational Problem: The Comparative Essay

The comparative essay is a special assignment. It is a challenging format that is often used for AP Exam questions and final course examination topics. The organization is not difficult as long as you keep in mind the comparative purpose of the paper. The pitfall is writing a comparative essay that never does any comparing — lots of information with no comparisons drawn between the halves. A history student, for example, asked to compare the programs set up to regulate business that were passed in the administration of Woodrow Wilson with those passed in the administration of Franklin D. Roosevelt, might recount all she knows about Wilson, then all she knows about Roosevelt, and then conclude. This is not a comparison.

One way to get it right is to discuss the first part of the comparison, in this case Wilson's regulatory programs; then construct the second half, Roosevelt's presidency, with constant *point-by-point* reference to what has already been said about Wilson. The second paragraph will include sentences such as the following:

> Roosevelt had opposition similar to that confronted by Wilson, but he employed different tactics to overcome it.

> But like Wilson, Roosevelt found his backers were fickle.

> These measures finally were more successful than what Wilson accomplished.

Proceed in sequence through your points, sticking with the order established in the first part of your essay but continually making comparative comments about similarities and differences. To win the opinion of your readers, the conclusion will carefully and methodically summarize all the comparisons discussed in the essay.

Another — better — method of organization, more likely to be used in an essay prepared outside of class than for an examination question, separates aspects of the comparison. In the example to the right below, the writer isolates individual aspects of the topic — creation of programs, implementation, obstacles, success, impact — and then looks at each president's handling of them. Here is a pair of outlines that shows the difference between the two ways of writing a comparison:

A. *Comparing Wilson and FDR*	B. *Comparing Wilson and FDR*
1. Wilson	1. Creation of programs
a. programs	a. Wilson
b. implementation	b. FDR
c. obstacles	2. Implementation
d. success	a. Wilson
e. impact	b. FDR
2. FDR (with reference to Wilson)	3. Obstacles
a. programs	a. Wilson
b. implementation	b. FDR
c. obstacles	4. Success
d. success	a. Wilson
e. impact	b. FDR
3. Comparative summary	5. Long-term impact
	a. Wilson
	b. FDR
	6. Short conclusion
	a. Wilson
	b. FDR

The second strategy does not necessarily cover more material than the first, but it is more directly comparative and more clearly organized. The reader can follow the comparisons easily and the conclusion doesn't have to do as much. Like a lot of things in life, the second way is harder ... but better!

Editing

Transition

Years ago, on an early nature program called *Wild Kingdom*, the host tried to create a strong transition between the show and the commercials:

> *That lion cub was almost eaten by those jackals. But luckily his father was there to protect him. You'll feel that same security when you're protected by (sponsor's name) insurance.*

Sometimes the stretch was a bit comical, but by repeating a key word (such as *protect*) and using demonstratives (*that, those*) and transitional expressions (*but*), the host established a connection between the program and the advertisements.

Transition is still the most important stylistic skill you can master. It is the way to create connections and coherence in your writing. It is absolutely essential to a smooth introduction, important within and especially at the beginning of body paragraphs, and helpful as you move into the conclusion.

There are three major ways to create transition:

Rule 1

Use transitional expressions. These words and phrases make connections wherever they appear:

To show time or sequence: first, second, then

To show cause: therefore, thus, hence

To show similarity: and, like, similarly, likewise

To show difference: on the other hand, however

Example: Ahab sees Moby Dick as his goal in life. *Likewise*, Jay Gatsby sees Daisy as his goal.

Rule 2

Repeat key words and sentence structure (parallelism).

Example: Ahab **sees** Moby Dick **as his goal** in life. Likewise, Jay Gatsby **sees** Daisy **as his goal**. (Note the repetition of the words "sees" and "goal" and the use of parallel sentence structure.)

Example: "... that government of **the people**, by the **people**, for the **people**, shall not perish from the earth." ("People" is repeated in a series of three prepositional phrases.)

Rule 3

Use pronouns (he, she, it, they) and demonstrative nouns and adjectives (this, that).

Example: Francis Bacon: "He that hath wife and children hath given hostages to fortune, for **they** are impediments to great enterprise. ..."

Example: Franklin D. Roosevelt: "The New Deal is our hope. **It** is the way to recovery. **It** is the immediate way. **It** is the strongest assurance that the recovery will endure."

The following paragraph relies heavily on transition to guide the reader. Notice the different methods used, particularly the paragraph hook that connects the next paragraph to this one.

Another way Melville makes the reader aware of the transition from sanity to insanity is in his imagery. Throughout the novel, he weaves a careful pattern of images that turn from normal to abnormal, from familiar to strange. For example, the images of fire begin in the friendly inns of Nantucket and New Bedford. Ishmael rejoices in the privilege of "making my own summer with my own coals" (61). Fire is here warmth and companionship. Even Queequeg's sacrificial fire to Yojo serves as the beginning of intimate friendship between the two sailors. But slowly this begins to change. By the middle of the novel, fire begins to suggest evil. It is associated with Ahab's mad purpose, what critic Richard Chase in *The American Novel and Its Tradition* calls "the self-absorption that leads to isolation, madness and suicide" (109). Ahab calls himself a volcano in "The Quarter-Deck" chapter and the crew swears death to Moby Dick in a fiery crossing of harpoons. Later, in the chapter called "The Tryworks," Ishmael compares the rendering fires to the fires of hell. By Chapter 113, hot-forged harpoons are being dipped

Word Repetition

Transitional Expressions

Pronouns and Demonstrative Adjective

Transitional
Expressions

Paragraph
Hook

Pronouns and
Demonstrative
Adjective

in blood as Ahab baptizes the crew *"in nomine diabolis"* (373). Nature's <u>fire</u>, lightning, warns the crew away by igniting the masts and nearly striking Ahab. The happy home<u>fires</u> of Nantucket have changed into the dangerous <u>fires</u> of Ahab's mad passion; (thus) they reinforce the novel's movement from sanity to insanity. (Like) Melville's <u>imagery</u>, <u>his</u> characters too move toward madness. (First) there is Pip . . . .

Try to keep transition in mind as you draft and especially as you revise your essay. It will provide the flow and cohesiveness that every essay needs.

Reviewing Your Draft

The grinding is over. Now for a little polishing. Readers gauge the care and commitment you've put into your essay by the thoroughness of this polishing. Proofread your essay carefully and slowly. You can enhance this process if you read your essay aloud. Look for:

FOCUS: Check for coherence throughout the essay. Can the reader find the main idea (thesis) and follow it from beginning to end? You might have someone read your introduction to see what he or she thinks your essay is about. If there's any doubt in the reader's mind, rework that paragraph. Then be sure your main idea is not only clear in your introduction but is referred to throughout the essay, especially at the beginning of body paragraphs.

PROOF: Make your claim seem like the only way to see things by developing each body paragraph with extensive, specific, and related evidence. This is the meat of the sandwich — make it substantial.

CORRECTNESS: Want to really impress the reader? Then proofread once *after* you've used the spelling and grammar checker. Spell-checkers won't notice highlight this kind of error. Don't be lazy about this. A recruiter told me she turned down a good job candidate because he'd misspelled the company name in his application letter: "He's careless; he'll only cause headaches for me and embarrassment sometime when it really matters." Right or wrong, we are often judged on small things.

In a second reading, consider *how* things are said, in addition to *what* you have said. Read with the eyes of an enemy looking for problems with your claim. Strengthen your evidence.

Set the essay aside for a few days — unless it's due tomorrow! (If it is, take this moment to resolve not to wait until the last minute next time.) When you think you are ready to look at your essay with a fresh, more objective eye, go back, reread it and make any changes that will improve your argument. Once you are satisfied, it is time for a little outside evaluation. Ask someone whose writing ability you respect to read your essay. The writing center at your school is a good option. Try to pick a reader whose comments aren't threatening to you so you can really hear what he or she is saying. Your boyfriend or girlfriend is probably not the best choice, either — too friendly to be a good critic.

Ultimately, you are the best editor. No one can speak for you; your own words and ideas are your best bet. Be sure to proofread the final draft several times yourself to eliminate unnecessary words and all errors in spelling, punctuation and grammar. Proofread, proofread, proofread!

Understanding and Avoiding Plagiarism

You've heard the word plagiarism but may not know precisely what it means. Taking someone else's words or ideas and presenting them as your own is a form of stealing called plagiarism. Quotations from *Hamlet* in a paper on *Hamlet* are the support for your theory. Words and ideas from critics who agree with you add credibility to your argument, whether you quote them directly or paraphrase their words. So identify in the text or by footnotes all direct quotations, paraphrases, and borrowed ideas. It doesn't matter whether the source is today's newspaper, an out-of-print book, a website, a YouTube clip, or a friend's research report; you are required to acknowledge the use of any borrowed material. You want your readers to see you as someone who knows and engages with the ideas of others. All this citing shows you are part of the conversation, the "spirited discourse" on the subject; you are contributing to a debate, helping search for new knowledge, trading in the marketplace of ideas. For complete rules on how to cite borrowed material, consult your English class handbook or the *MLA Handbook for Writers of Research Papers* (listed in Suggested Reading at the end of this book).

Reviewing the Process

The Essay: The written defense of a thesis or claim

An Introduction: offers a road map or an invitation to the claim

1. The Road Map Introduction
   Claim
   Major Points
   End Sentence

Or you may choose:

2. The General-to-Specific Introduction
   A General Statement in the Topic Area
   Increasingly Specific Statements
   Thesis

The Body: presents an ordered sequence of evidence for the claim

A series of paragraphs that each follow this pattern:
   Topic Sentence (states topic of paragraph, shows relation of
      paragraph to claim, may show transition from the previous paragraph)
   Development (extensive specific examples and evidence to
      support your thesis ... about 80 percent of each paragraph)
   End Sentence (optional especially in a short paragraph)

A Conclusion: summarizes or speculates

1. Summary Conclusion
   Claim
   Major Points
   End Sentence

Or you may choose:

2. Speculative Conclusion
   Claim
   Short Summary of Essay
   New but Related Point (generalization, speculation, judgment,
   recommendation)

The essay process begins with the gathering of ideas by brainstorming, a process that should result in a specific thesis and a simple outline. This can take three minutes during a final examination or several weeks in the preparation of a research paper. Depending on the length and complexity of the topic, you may or may not want to refine and expand the simple outline as you continue to plan, research, and prepare.

Once you're writing, create an introduction that makes your thesis clear (the introduction can also make your whole essay plan clear). The body is the proof and should be a careful selection of points that validate your thesis. A conclusion does its job well when it sums up what you've said; it may also raise further possibilities.

Keep your style simple and create transitions between ideas and between paragraphs.

Edit your work yourself and with some outside help. You will probably want to consult a writing handbook for some of the fine points of style, grammar, research, and footnoting. Check Suggested Reading in the back of this book for the names of some helpful reference books. Save your document and back it up (no, really). Then print a final copy, proofread it a few times, and electronically submit; you can feel satisfied at having followed a process through from beginning to end.

The essay is a marvelously flexible form. Its only strict requirements are a clear and continual focus and plenty of proof. "Tell 'em what you're gonna tell 'em, tell 'em, tell 'em what you told 'em." Use a beginning to present your thesis, a middle full of persuasive evidence, and an end that returns to and reaffirms the thesis.

The advice in this chapter is not intended to be an inflexible set of dos and don'ts for writing. These are suggestions, beginnings; some you will always use, some you will outgrow. All are designed to put you in control of your own writing.

Toolbox: More Editing Tips

1. A simple style is best. Good writing sounds like speech rather than a vocabulary review lesson. Where you are having problems expressing an idea, try using shorter sentences and simpler words rather than longer sentences and a thesaurus.

2. Evaluate your writing for sentence variety. Write some long, complex sentences. Then be brief. An occasional short sentence adds impact. And consider beginning some sentences with a phrase or clause, rather than relying always on the subject or the same word (application essays often suffer from too many sentences that begin with "I").

3. Remember your audience and the requirements of the assignment. There are differences in the structure, style, and precision required in a science journal entry versus a finished lab report, in an essay for your drama class versus a final term paper in a Shakespeare seminar for senior English majors.

4. In general:

   • Reconsider those dashes and exclamation points. They are the junk food of the punctuation world, a bit too casual or hysterical for the tone of most essays. Apply sparingly.

   • Avoid parentheses. Perhaps a little reorganization is in order. And an ugly truth: a lot of readers skip what's in the parentheses.

   • Ask questions sparingly. Asking them seems a little contrived if you intend to answer the questions yourself.

   • Rewrite any expressions you're tempted to place in sanitizing quotation marks. "Monet was really 'into' water lilies" is a mismatch of style and substance. And it's unclear what you mean. Think a little more and choose a different word: "Monet found water lilies fascinating."

   • Avoid contractions, abbreviations, and slang. Keep your style restrained and scrupulously correct.

As in everything, there are usage conventions and somewhat arbitrary rules of formality. Most academic writing requires that you observe these conventions, although each audience will be a little different and each teacher may have his or her own pet peeves. Usually these are explained early in a course or described in the writing handbook recommended by the teacher.

chapter 4

What's the Question?

Applying to college has changed. It's a whole new world. Or at least this is the claim you will find in a small explosion of articles every August. New rules, new systems, new results. And doubtless there are adjustments every year — but hardly the revolution journalists claim. Institutions of higher education remain committed to the best interests of their student body, they apply abundant time and funds to the process of identifying individuals who will benefit by the opportunities they offer, they work with near religious commitment to fairness and thoroughness, and in the end, with very few exceptions, make rational, justifiable, and even explainable decisions about access. Are mistakes made? Are injustices done? Maybe. But on the whole, the business of applying and being admitted to college has been and remains a fair sequence of judgments that offers access to education to every well-qualified and committed student.

Where are the changes then? In the numbers. More students are applying to college and a greater percentage of the population now attends college. Add grade inflation to this and it's harder for colleges to differentiate among applicants. Colleges want to provide a broad-based experience for their students. More first-generation students, more geographic diversity, more nontraditional students are part of that plan. "Nothing is a safety school," says Jennifer Fondiller, dean of admissions at Barnard College, "because nothing is by the numbers now."

Parental panic has set in and the myths and strategies proliferate. I asked one Ivy League dean: "Ten years ago, parents wondered if they should switch their clarinet-playing son to oboe to improve his chances of admission to college. Is that still going on?" "Not at all," he said. "Now it's bassoon."

And of course, costs have risen. Not too much more than the CPI — a year of college still costs about the same as a luxury automobile with a bunch of the standard options. (You'll pay what I paid for college if you buy a big new TV.) But while a high school student's summer job might have earned a decent percentage of a year's tuition when college cost $3,000/year, this isn't possible in today's economy. Costs for colleges themselves have increased — computer help desks, Title IX requirements, and gluten-free vegetarian dining options did not exist in 1975.

The Common Application

So it is easy to write those "It's a Whole New Ballgame" articles every fall. But it is worth it to remember that the admission system itself remains a fairly unchanged process of evaluation and selection. You aren't signing up to play Russian roulette with the rest of your education. It's a clear, well-articulated process, and if there has been change, most of it is for the better: gender equity, minority access, international populations, help centers, new dorms, fewer fraternities. Another example of change for the better is the rise of the Common Application.

A century ago, a letter of application written by a potential student and endorsed by well-connected friends might be all that was required. After the Second World War, when veterans returned to join the applicant pool, a more regularized process evolved, and applicants filled out forms provided by the colleges. In 1975, first based at Vassar College and two years later through the administrative efforts of the National Association of Secondary School Principals, the Common Application was born. Over the last 40 years, this form has made life simpler for applicants. Today more than 500 colleges share an application used by close to a million students.

The Common Application has always included an essay. Twenty years ago, there were three essay options. Today there are more, but the questions, surprisingly, have not changed much. A defining experience, an important moment, an achievement ... the essay questions share a fairly basic assumption: Insight can be gained if the applicant chooses a focus and gives evidence to explain the choice. Good news, huh? That's what we've been talking about. An essay makes a claim. Then it offers support for that claim. The Common Application asks you to choose an event in your life and prove it was significant, fruitful, defining. And the essay prompts of non-Common Application schools aren't very different. They don't ask for a one-act play or a sonnet or new lyrics to "My Country 'Tis of Thee." They ask for evidence about a claim on a topic you are deeply familiar with ... all good news.

Individual colleges may ask for additional supplemental essays and responses. These requirements are found in the Writing Supplements or Questions section of each school's application — accessed from the school's website or on the Common Application website — and they vary from a simple request for information about why you've chosen to apply ("What motivated you to apply to Rice University?") to a request for your favorite word, your design for an ideal course, or a description of a time when you "majored in unafraid" (Barnard). There is also the opportunity to upload Additional Information: "Please provide an answer below if you wish to provide details of circumstances or qualifications not reflected in the application. You may enter up to 650 words."

The Personal Essay of the Common Application

Not all colleges accept the Common Application. And of course it is possible to apply to college without having to write any essays at all. Many schools find that grades and scores provide adequate information to support their decisions. But on the assumption that the applications before you require essays and that at least one of the colleges uses the Common Application, let's take a look at what you are about to undertake. Surprisingly, I'd like to suggest that this is not by any means an overwhelming challenge. In fact, I would claim that no matter how many schools you apply to, you are only going to have to write one essay — an answer to the question "Tell us about yourself."

Let's pretend for a moment that "Tell us about yourself" is the question. (It used to be Yale's application essay question.) If you remember that you are the "text" here, you are the book or the war or the biology experiment under discussion, a question like "Tell us about yourself" asks you to reach into a complex body of information and choose an enlightening bit. In school essays, you chose a scene, a battle, or a seedling's growth and then illuminated the larger subject by a lens or optic on this smaller selection. Asked to tell about yourself, you should do the same: a day in the life, a special conversation that changed your outlook, a success or failure that inspired your efforts. Not so difficult — it's the same process described in Chapter 3: focus and prove.

The questions in the essay portion of most applications and on the Common Application itself are quite a bit easier than "Tell us about yourself" (perhaps explaining Yale's decision to drop that question). The questions seek a sense of who you are and offer a lens through which to show that: an event, a location, an experience, an issue. They are saying, "Use a book you love, a risk you took, an event you care about, a time everything went wrong, to tell us about yourself." They are easing the process but focusing your selection. "Don't tell us everything ... use something small and illuminating to show us something we need to know about something large and complicated — YOU."

Consider the curator of the local history museum. She's been offered funding for an exhibition to commemorate the anniversary of the Wright brothers' flight at Kitty Hawk. Certainly this was a significant event in the history of flight. And flight progress has been remarkable from that North Carolina beach to the moon and Mars. But what to include? The Smithsonian might lend some Wright brothers' letters about the test flight. Interesting … maybe. There are drawings of the plane. That's more like it. And there's a crazy, jerky bit of black-and-white film footage that records the triumphant moment. Okay, now she's on to something. Selection. There are lots of things to choose from; in the end, the exhibition will comprise the items the curator believes vividly light up the brief event that transformed transportation history.

You can illuminate your personality and preferences through an issue as small as your annoying older brother or as grand as the instability of the Eurozone's economies.

But, any and all questions share the same goal: an effort by the colleges to get a look at you as a writer, of course, but also as a chooser, a reflective and insightful person able to select one element and use it as a lens for viewing that complicated thing called YOU. Hence my claim that there is only one question.

Every application essay question is a variation of the question "Tell us about yourself" tricked out in a different guise: "Tell us about yourself … using an event, a work of art, a feature of your own diversity, a failure, a letter to your future roommate."

Writing Supplements

Once you've put together that core essay, the presentation of "yourself" through an illuminating lens, you're not quite done. You've completed the work for many of the schools that accept the Common Application; it's likely that you've done most of the thinking needed for an essay at any of the non-Common Application schools, as well. But there's still some work to do. Many schools ask for additional essays meant to enrich your core presentation and add to their understanding of your writing skill. These questions "brand" the school a bit and assess your knowledge of the school in question. The questions can be quite straightforward: "Briefly discuss your reasons for applying to Colby?" Many are more creative: "In the space below … briefly think out loud about something that's been on your mind for awhile" (Bennington College).

Here are some additional samples:

"Describe an experience that sparked your interest in mathematics, science, or engineering." (Harvey Mudd College)

"Please tell us how you have spent the last two summers …" (Princeton University)

"Tell us about a time when you were in the minority." (Eugene Lang College)

"What factors have led you to consider Macalester College?"

"Why NYU?"

"Please tell us what academic class has been your favorite and why." (Columbia University)

Again, I suggest that there remains essentially only one question: "Tell us about yourself." All of the above samples share the same goal and therefore are manageable through the same strategy: focus and prove. Just as the Common Application asks for a choice or experience as a lens into your character and personality, these questions do the same: experience, summer, class. All of these are preselected lenses for your response.

essential to share that doesn't appear in your essays, credentials, the letters from your teachers, or in the composite recommendation from your school counselor. This might be the place to put a link to your YouTube violin solo with the local philharmonic or to direct the reader to a SlideRoom arts submission. "If there is a hanging question out there, answer it," says Tara Dowling, former college counselor at Üsküdar American Academy in Istanbul. "But there needs to be a compelling reason to include the information. Not every story needs to be told." Is there a gap in your education, a sudden transfer of schools, a medical situation, or a surprising grade in a course you've always excelled in? Be sure the information isn't apparent from the comments of others. And be sure it's really essential information. If you have a B average in science and received a C in physics ... well, they'll get that. It's physics, for goodness sake! And if you've suffered a string of setbacks, you might ask your counselor to speak to that. You have put it all behind you, hopefully, and are ready for college. The best proof of that is that you didn't bother to obsess about it in your essay. Jennifer Fondiller at Barnard points out, "Admission offices are starting to be overwhelmed with additional information and support materials." Choose wisely and remember not every space provided needs to be filled.

The School Paper

Some colleges require or encourage you to upload an academic essay or writing sample. This element makes sense since, as you saw in Chapter 3, a lot of college writing is similar to what is done in high school. Choose a strong performance (a B + or better) and a paper on a not-too-esoteric topic. Do not send a 15-page term paper or a collation of library research; the schools that require this will guide you about length and selection. A short, illuminating essay on one poem, one lab experiment, or one incident in history is a good choice. Poetry and creative writing might be options as well, but unless you've won an award or received some other type of outside encouragement for your work, stick with a good expository school essay.

Scholarship and Program Essays

As you complete the application process, there are several other opportunities to "speak for yourself" and advocate for your cause in your writing. You may have scored so well on the PSAT/NMSQT that you have qualified as a finalist. Your scores will be supported by an essay as the winners of scholarships are chosen.

Or you may be applying to a special program or source of funding at the college of your choice. The Chancellor's Scholarship and other monetary awards at Vanderbilt University require additional essays. Several large universities offer a small-class experience to those who qualify with exceptional grades and a great application essay. The Honors Program of Michigan's College of Literature, Science, and the Arts requires a support essay written after you are admitted. If you apply for an abroad program or a guest semester off-campus, you will write yet another "Why?" essay that explains both your motivation and the special features of the program important to your study and/or career plans. At Harvard, a personal statement or essay is required for admission to some of the popular Freshman Seminars.

Whatever work you put in on your college application essays will form a good foundation for this business of writing self-recommendations, which is what these kinds of essays really are. And the strategy is always the same. Decide what the school or institution needs to know about you; then prove that you would be an asset to the community. Focus and prove.

Five Key Concepts About the Application Essay

1. There's only one prompt: "Tell us about yourself."
2. OK ... there are actually two: "Tell us about yourself" and "Why do you wish to attend University X?" You'll need to be able to answer no. 1 to do a good job with no. 2.
3. Whatever the challenge, in every case, you are the authority on the topic.
4. The format is not unfamiliar; it's a regular essay with "you" as the text.
5. This is not a punishment — it's a chance to add life to your application, to pitch yourself outside the numbers, to show you know what you're doing, and to file a request that says "Pick me!"

Toolbox: Cyber Sense

General websites like www.collegeboard.com, financial aid sites like www.fafsa.ed.gov, or the site for downloading the Common Application (www.commonapp.org) are wonderful resources. The sites of the colleges themselves provide names and numbers, deadlines, tour information, maps, downloadable forms, and extensive program information. Current students blog on various topics, a program pioneered at Johns Hopkins University. You can follow the college on Twitter or view news on the Facebook page. On most of these sites, you can email questions from the "Contact Us" page or find the right coach or faculty member to query.

There are an equal number of websites with more commercial intent — lots of places to find advisement, tutorials, and "tips." Let the counseling program at your school be your first and consistent source of information. TMI can certainly apply to the college search, and websites that aggregate the anxiety and ignorance of a large population of freaked-out parents and kids is not a place you want to visit. And there are plenty of essays to download if you think you don't really need to write this yourself. That would mean giving up the opportunity to present all that's interesting about you — and offering a stale bit of someone else for your voice of advocacy. Not a good idea. Also not legal — see the note on plagiarism at the end of Chapter 3 if you have any questions about this.

Many schools offer seniors the convenience of gathering their data in one place on Naviance. There are a multitude of useful tools and resources included in the Naviance package as well as on the Common Application site. And the ease of drafting essays on your computer as well as submitting them online simplifies the business of completing applications. If you have followed the timeline suggested in Chapter 2 and are not working against an immediate deadline, your idea bank is on a computer. Brainstorming may be a lot easier with a keyboard and screen than with pencil and paper, and any assignment benefits from the revision and editing capabilities of a computer.

Completing one version of the Common Application prepares you to file online to a multitude of colleges. Just remember that there is only one version of the application, with the allowance for two small-scale revisions to the essay. Don't reference a particular school in the main body of the application ("… my soccer experience will only improve once I'm playing for Michigan"), as only the supplements can be school-specific. Save your work and backup your efforts on a disk or thumb-drive every time you work on the essays. You can, of course, save your Common App work an unlimited number of times before you hit Submit. (I'm not sure why there's more stress in that moment than in running to the mailbox with a bunch of chubby envelopes, but I guess this is how technology reminds us that the machines are in charge.)

Final words of caution:

As you are drafting, keep your cursor off Word Count. If you are zipping up there every few minutes, you are clearly trying to flog a dead horse over the finish line. Choose a new topic. You should easily be able to write 850 words and edit to a tight 650 if you've chosen your topic wisely. The next chapter will show you how.

Budget your time and proofread carefully. Revising your Bryn Mawr essay for Wellesley is a poor idea if you forget to delete references to the advantages of living in the Philadelphia area. And while formatted pages tend to look perfect, often they are not.

Read drafts several times. Thorny problem areas that might have been identifiable by the multiple cross-outs and arrows of a written draft disappear on a computer screen. Read the essay copy on the screen but then print and proofread a final hard-copy draft before hitting Submit. The typographical errors that can be generated by a computer are reformatting problems, incomplete deletions, word substitutions ("form" for "from"), and misplaced insertions. Look for them.

Chapter 5

What's the Answer?

This chapter is the HOW.

The first step is to shift your thinking a bit. You may be thinking many applications = many essays. Not to worry. As suggested in Chapter 4, there is only one essay because there is only one topic: "Tell us about yourself." And while there are a number of things you might want to tell the school about yourself, the list is considerably shortened by the presence of your transcript, your recommendations, and the rest of your application materials.

If you are using the Common Application, your immediate challenge is very manageable: a personal essay on the "yourself" topic. There will be supplements for individual schools. Down the road, these can seem to be putting you in a scene from *The Birds* — many tiny, evil predators just waiting for you to set foot in their realm. But for the moment, you are contemplating a reasonable and familiar assignment about a familiar topic — you to date, in 650 words.

But let's not start with the questions. Let's start with the answers.

Building an Idea Bank

Look In

Your best friend just called. She's coming over. And 11 other friends have decided to flash mob your house, too. And they're hungry. Now you can sit at the kitchen table and fret over whether Josh is a vegetarian and whether dessert will be required. Or you can go over to the fridge, cruise through the cupboards, and take careful stock of what's on hand. If you happen to have two party-size lasagnas in the freezer (or the phone number of a good pizza joint that delivers), you're good to go. Likewise, before you spend time pondering any of the questions, you need to put in some time looking at what you have to work with. LOOK IN. Inventory the "cupboard of you." If you can pull together a list of reflections and facts about yourself, give it some shape, and save it as a file (ideally over several weeks, but several hours will do), you will have an idea bank from which you can make useful withdrawals no matter what the questions are.

Ask Questions

Start by brainstorming. Sit down at your computer and fill a screen with statements about yourself. You can start with things you've done, places you've been, accomplishments you're proud of. But those are just to get you going. Think about yourself, your values, choices you've made, mistakes or regrets you have, failures, surprises, changes of heart. If you're a reluctant writer, set a timer or a time limit and write for half an hour. Write down everything you can think of about yourself: the good, the bad, the special, the obvious, the habitual, the extraordinary. Don't consider your audience at this point. This performance is just for you.

Short on ideas? You might want to research your topic a little. There aren't any Cliffs Notes, and there's nothing in the public library. But you may have kept a diary or collected thoughts about your experiences. Or the resume you created for your school counselor or recommending teachers might yield some inspiration. What's on your smartphone? A quick tour through some family photograph albums or your online photo collections can be inspiring, too. If you have followed the plan in Chapter 2, you have a journal to review. Just don't get distracted from making this list and making it long.

Now ask some questions: "What are my strengths? My weaknesses?" Do a little soul-searching and be as complete as possible. Add evaluative statements like "I am a stubborn person" or "I like a challenge." Be totally honest. Why do you do the things you do? What drives you out the front door at 6 a.m. to run five miles? What keeps you up past midnight trying to build that crazy app?

Ask: What is different about me? What kind of person am I? Under what circumstances do I learn? What interests me? What's my favorite website, YouTube, TED talk? What do I care about? Why is swimming, to me, more a religion than a sport? What is it like growing up in Jerome, Idaho ... or Maplewood, New Jersey ... or Glendale, Missouri? How did I choose my Facebook picture? Whose Twitter feeds do I follow ... and why? What's my desktop background? Begin well in advance if you can. Let your ideas marinate.

Here's part of a former prompt from Tufts that encourages similar thinking:

"… consider the world within. Taste in music, food and clothing can make a statement while politics, sports, religion and ethnicity are often defining attributes. Are you a vegetarian? A poet? Do you prefer YouTube or test tubes, Mac or PC? Are you the drummer in an all-girl rock band? Do you tinker?"

These days, they are asking "What makes you happy?" Basically, Tufts is asking you to sort yourself out in the same way I am encouraging here. The end of high school is a natural juncture in any life. Even without the pressure of college applications, it is well worth the time to figure out what you believe in, where you excel, and what you want to do that is driven *not* by well-intentioned parental suggestion or cultural pressure but by your own interest. Because only your own interest will endure. Thus, a special fringe benefit of taking the college essay seriously is that it can be a learning experience, not just for the college, but for you.

Try sorting your responses into categories: academic interests, personal qualities, achievements (because, of course, you will be unable to resist making this a list of things you've done), ways you are connected to the world around you. Think: my mind, my heart, my actions, my world. But remember this is not a resume, not a list of achievements or activities. It is a bank of reflections about what you've thought and what you care about and who you are.

A first list might look like this:

1. Friends, especially Sabrina
2. Maplewood
3. My parents, Jason [brother], Delano [beloved dog]
4. School, especially physics (ugh)
5. U. S. history — love that class
6. The whole phys. ed. requirement thing — why?
7. Chorus
8. This summer — the choir trip
9. Volunteering at the Community House

Aim for two pages of items, maybe 300 words, good and bad, reflected on or just spat out. The first effort will drift toward events and feel like the drafting of a resume. But in fact you are trying to pull together a much broader and "softer" list of things about yourself.

Save as a file. Now go do something else. "Begun is half-done"; so, good for you.

Unpack

Another day, another time, try to organize and expand all this a bit. Add additional information. Look for clusters. The time between Step One and Step Two will have inspired more thoughts and reflections. Include more questions about some of your list items. And shape the list not by event or incident but by *personal characteristics*.

1. I like young kids
   a. my little brother
   b. babysitting: Andrew (a funny kid)
   c. Community House work
   d. Christmas pageant for the church — too many angels — should it be just for 4th graders?
   e. I'm interested in child psychology and why kids behave the way they do

2. Classes I like
   a. Mr. Stivers's U. S. history class
   b. music workshop
   c. Ms. Kochman's class — except I'm not getting an A there. Why?
   d. Is it physics or Mr. Buckley or 7:45 a.m. that makes me want to be sick every first period?

3. I do really hate sports
   a. gym is dumb — we never do anything so why is that required?
   b. in fourth grade I never got picked for a team
   c. the athletes are pretty stuck on themselves (all that game day stuff)
   d. I've got enough competition in my life already
   e. I'm uncoordinated (falling off the parallel bars in 6th grade in front of Justin)

4. I always put things off until right before the deadline
   a. this essay
   b. my 10th-grade research paper
   c. getting my yearbook quote done
   d. prom table? Do we have to do that now?

5. Growing up in Maplewood
    a. nice
    b. a lot of people commute to New York
    c. is it different from the Midwest or California?
    d. what was Hartford like? we moved when I was six — first grade
    e. St. George's

Making more connections is the next step. You need to analyze your topic and divide it into manageable pieces. As you saw in *The Simpsons* sample in Chapter 3, grouping similar ideas and events together highlights patterns in a miscellaneous collection of information. For example, is there a series of volunteer projects? Does your love of music show up in your performance but also in your work on the church pageant? Does technology matter to you enough to send you to the state science competition and also across the street to your neighbor who can't seem to make her printer work? Ask yourself more questions to establish connections, clusters, and groups. Think: my mind, my heart, my actions, my world.

Nominate

Time to focus. You are only going to need two to three ideas for all your essays, and only one for the core essay of this "'Tell us about yourself" kind. Choose three or four personal strengths or characteristics. Don't choose an event. The least productive counseling sessions begin when a senior says, "I'm going to write about my trip to X" or "My essay is going to be about football." Your thinking should begin with "I'm going to write about my curiosity" or "My essay is about my creativity." Be positive — "stubborn" isn't quite the thing, but "committed" works. And don't be afraid of the truth; being honest is the only way to get a fresh and sincere result.

There's an opportunity here for a little input. Don't ask your friends "What should I write my essay about?" But if you haven't done this already, ask your parents (and then maybe friends) what they think are your most outstanding qualities. Stay away from "things that have happened" and try to get some inspiration about how you function in the world — what you love, what you value, how you make decisions. Find some things that the admissions office needs to know about you that are missing from your application.

The Common Application says this with true directness: "What do you want the readers of your application to know about you apart from courses, grades, and test scores?" Stanford's instructions share the same spirit: "What matters to you, and why?" Yale has asked: "While we leave the topic of the second essay entirely up to you, try telling us something about yourself that you believe we cannot learn elsewhere in your application." Keep this advice as the measure by which you sort and settle your topic choices. Nominate these ideas as the potential claim of your core application essay.

Nominations:

1. Not competitive in sports but competitive in class

2. Full of questions about how kids develop, learn to behave, experience the world

3. A procrastinator — why?

4. I like to talk in class — probably contribute 3–4x day in history (but never in physics?)

Find the Lens

Okay. Now you are ready to think about this as an essay rather than a self-inventory. Your purpose is to show the readers a particular view or interpretation of your subject, to reveal and make vivid a side of yourself that appears nowhere else in the application. What makes a great paper on *The House on Mango Street* will make a great essay on you: a clear claim and solid evidence. The first requires specific quotations and references from the novel. The college essay requires evidence from your life.

Keep asking questions but try to organize your information in clusters that relate. List personality characteristics, and under each one list five or six thoughts or bits of evidence from your life, things you've been or done, that relate. Each characteristic is a potential focus for your core essay, and you need to see which ones are important, which ones "have legs" and which are dead ends.

The evidence is crucial. If you've said you're concerned with how kids learn and develop but can't think of more than one experience that exposed you to that, omit it. It's not a major thread. Maybe your Dad thought that one up or maybe you thought you *ought* to be interested in that. But if there's no trail of bread crumbs leading to that little house, then you aren't going to be able to find your way back to reality. You're being tempted by the witch of "what I ought to think." Instead, as you might toy with opinions about a novel's characters, setting, or foreshadowing techniques, experiment with ideas about your own goals, interests, or style. Then see what things have happened to you and what you have done that supports or illuminates these preliminary "me/thesis statements."

Time for more questions. About which items on your list have you written the most? What looks interesting, different (but not unflattering)? Are there any career goals here? Motivations for college? Special personal characteristics or experiences? Working with kids might be interesting if your career and college choice are related. The preference for classes with student participation might make a good essay in applying to a college with seminar classes. Certainly a loathing for sports is an interesting point. But where can you go with it? Can you use it to show something positive about yourself — maybe your individuality? — rather than eccentricity or negativity? The procrastination habit is probably not something you want to share with the college. But it might be if you have some interesting insights or ways you've learned to manage that.

There are no right answers for these questions any more than for any other essay. Admission committees are diverse groups of individuals; there isn't one particular thing they want to hear. After reading 20 to 50 essays a day about the charms of University X, the evils of terrorism, and the personal commitment involved in being a doctor, most admission staffers don't want more essays on "safe" topics. How things are in Skokie, Illinois, or New Hope, Alabama, might be more engaging. Your little brother Jason is worthy of some reflection. And how much you've figured out about your own half-competitive/half-collaborative self would be very welcome. The importance of protecting the environment? They know that. Passionate avowals of your love for University X's gorgeous autumnal foliage? Not so much. "Schools would rather have a sense of the student's place in the world, a sense of his or her relationship — context — as a person," says Chicago-based educational consultant Betsy DeLaHunt.

Bates' Bill Hiss agrees, "We don't want the back lot at MGM, a created scene over a barren field. We want to see the real landscape." So be full of thoughts ... but be full of *your* thoughts. Looking for the "right" answers is pointless and undercuts the intention here. Massachusetts Institute of Technology advises:

"You should certainly be thoughtful about your essays but if you're thinking too much — spending a lot of time stressing or strategizing about what makes you 'look best' as opposed to the answers that are honest and easy — you're doing it wrong."

So put in the time on this idea bank, your nominations, your list of evidence, your options. Play around with the inclusions. And revert to the opinions of others as little as possible. When you start to talk "essay" with your family, your counselor, and your friends, they will be full of ideas. But suddenly all YOUR ideas will disappear and you will be thrown left and right by advice. Thyra Briggs at Harvey Mudd speaks about this problem: "Too much advice and you end up removing yourself from the essay. That's a mistake. You end up writing 'Innovation is important.' What you mean to say is 'Space travel is cool—let me tell you why.'"

Hold onto that original list of thoughts, ideas, and events and visit it often. Don't cheat on this step and don't give it away. Write to write. It will be money in the bank for the next investment of time.

The Questions

Once you have a handful of possible claims you'd like to make, ideas about yourself you'd like to share, it is finally time to look at the questions. Again, each question varies only in turning the angle of vision a little to the left or right: tell us about yourself through a central life story, tell us about yourself through a failure, a brave moment, an accomplishment. But there are a few considerations you should be aware of as you decide which lens will shine the strongest light on you.

1. If you choose a significant event, this is a straightforward request for a selection from your life that you consider a "hot spot," a moment to notice and remember. The challenge in this question is the business of significance. They aren't asking for just any event. It has to be important. What does that require? Does someone have to die? Should there be trauma involved? When I worked in admissions, I regularly lobbied for quite a different question: "Tell us about an **insignificant** experience and make us believe it was significant." So your lens here is almost any event in your life that you've pondered and reflected on. Your focus will be to show your interpretive ability and a bit of your value system as you choose a focus and unfold for the reader the impact. The event doesn't need to be "significant" in any culturally marked way — divorce, death, a Purple Heart, a donated kidney — are not required. What will make or break this topic is your ability to show/prove the significance of the event. Your Dad drove you through his hometown once. It took about half an hour. Not significant. He told you what his world was like and you wondered if you had any motivations as strong as his. Okay — that's significant. You study four hours a night. Not a big deal, really. That studying produces a string of C+'s. We can see that on the transcript. Your brother, however, never studies at all and receives straight A's ... that's worth reflecting on. One instruction suggests: "Tell us your thoughts. The choice of event should be driven by what you want us to know about you after we've read your narrative."

2. Some essay questions narrow the field and ask you to choose a controversy or political issue; here again, the tail wags this dog. This essay will win or lose on your ability to prove the issue matters to you, that you've thought a lot about it, and that you can make the reader believe this is, regardless of its front-page newsworthy status, important to you. This question is intended to "tell us about yourself" through an issue you care about. You might think it needs to be Eurozone debt, but it doesn't. It could be the condition of the high school football field or even something as small and personal as your procrastination habit. Be an authority on something and win.

3. If you have declared an area of interest on your application, some schools want to hear about an academic project or experience related to this interest. Again, be specific (see the sample on p. 89). Help the reader see why you love biology or French. Your enthusiasm and depth of involvement in the project are most important. Your work does not have to have earned a prize — or even an A. It needs to connect to what you will be able to pursue further at the college or university that asks this question. So look at their course offerings and the depth of faculty in your area of interest — see if you can find what their seniors are working on. The college would love to hear how active and interesting you will be once you arrive.

4. Some schools ask you to choose a person who has had a significant influence on you; the key here is the word "influence." You can choose St. Augustine or Tina Fey. But your essay will work best if you choose according to the personal characteristic about yourself that you've decided to convey. Your curiosity? Then the Kardashians are probably not as suitable as Kim Jong-un. Your creativity? Damien Hirst or your high school theater director but probably not your older brother (unless he's Damien Hirst). There are no right or wrong answers, just persuasive and revealing answers about you as opposed to generic and unconvincing ones not about you. "The danger here," says Julie Browning at Rice University, "is an essay all about that other person." So the influence cannot just be asserted. If you say, "From him I have learned to let my spirit soar," show the reader where and when that spirit was soaring. Have you published something, painted something, put together an impressive project as a result of this influence? "Let your life preach." Your reader will be convinced — and will know more about achievements that may not appear elsewhere in the application — if you can prove your claim and show evidence of the influence.

5. If you are asked to choose an important book or creative work (an in art, music, science, etc.), see no. 3 above … keeping in mind that this question is similar but more difficult. While others often inspire our actions, books, art and people we've never met are another matter. Is it possible that reading *The Girl with the Dragon Tattoo* has made you the person you are today? Here's the proof of the

difficulty of gauging influence: When John Ruskin claimed his vision as an art critic was galvanized one day on a trip to Fontainebleau, he was in his 80s. His diaries surfaced a half-century later, and critics examined the pages for the dates on which he made this storied trip. No mention of the life-shaping event was to be found. The diary said something like "Went to Fontainebleau. Sat under a tree." It takes a few decades to know what has shaped your life. Showing you've made the transition from childhood to adulthood, for example, is a pretty big assignment. How your reading and arts experiences have made you the 17-year-old you are is even more tricky. Spend your time thinking (and then writing) about the evidence of the change; this is more important than the book or event you choose.

6. If you are asked how you will contribute to the diversity in a college community, you need to make a claim for your own distinctiveness and demonstrate a good understanding of how your experiences differ from those of others. Remember that all the applicants are teenagers and they are for the most part presently enrolled in a high school somewhere. So real distinctions aren't going to be easy. Here's the beginning of a reasonable effort:

> My high school is sixty-nine percent white. My town is eighty-five percent white. I live in an affluent, liberal community that stresses racial diversity and acceptance. But every day, on the way to my Spanish class, I pass a bulletin board on the third floor labeled "High Achieving Students of Color." Fifteen names and photographs are posted there. It is meant to be an honor commending accomplished students. I study the pictures. I wonder if the board is somehow undercutting the work of those it means to praise. The students look proud. Am I over-reacting, overanalyzing a blameless deed? I wonder if the 15 students even have an answer . . .

It's a start, and the author is raising interesting questions about an encounter she has every day in her school. More needs to be said here; more thinking should be conveyed. But already the reader has a sense of someone who will take a risk, who likes to kick ideas around, challenge the accepted norms, and test the truth of the assumptions of others — someone whose life probably isn't remarkable but someone who is ready to take advantage of the opportunities of a college curriculum.

7. A word about mistakes and failures: some essay prompts ask for one or the other of these. Remember they are not the same thing. A failure is an effort that did not succeed; your focus should be to make it very, very clear that this play, or this fund-raiser, or this bid to be captain came to nothing. Be specific. You only raised $75 and $50 came from your Dad. That's important. Second,

you need to tease apart why things came to nothing...and only briefly at the end address how you've modified your behavior based on this disaster. The majority of the response should be details about the failure and reflections on those details.

Conversely, a mistake is an error of judgment, almost always the result of incomplete knowledge. This question allows you to explore what you didn't know, but it is usually more focused than the request for an essay about a failure.

Be careful about pasting one college's required supplement into another school's application. I remind you of this danger here because requests for failures are not requests for mistakes. And eccentric supplement questions are on-offs. Pasting Brandeis's "Imagine you have to wear a costume for a year of your life" sent off as a half-answer to "Discuss an example of a question, skill, or ability [my ability to dress as Superman for a year] that you've explored or would like to explore outside the classroom" is a bad idea.

8. Several college supplements require a personal letter of introduction. Stanford, for example, asks you to "write a note to your future roommate." They're not kidding. Your response should sound like a note from one teenager to another. (Even if you don't have this question on your list, it's a great first question to fool around with because it forces you to stay "real," to sound like yourself.) Cover lots of ground and provide lots of personal detail. If you don't include your preferences for a future Half X/Half Y pizza, you're not finished with this one.

The Common Application and the colleges themselves constantly modify and refine the questions they ask, looking for ways that applicants can offer a piece of writing that will convey a solid sense of who they are. The board of the Common Application wants the options to be as broad and far-ranging as possible. Don't worry if the questions are new every year — they will never be very far from "Tell us about yourself." Carry on as long as your response fulfills the requirements outlined here — as long as it conveys a characteristic about yourself not evident from the rest of the application and supports that choice with specific detail.

Off to a Bad Start

Throughout my high school years, there have been many factors that have influenced my interests and personality. Being a well-rounded student, I have had many experiences working with people as well as with books. I have learned a great deal through these experiences. Another major influence in my life has been my family. Their love and encouragement have motivated me to expand in many areas of *interest. I have been influenced by my involvement in many activities outside of academics ...*

Oh dear. The clear indication that this is a very weak start is that almost every single person reading this sample could cut and paste the material into their own application essay. If your essay is supposed to tell the reader about you, help admissions see the complex and interesting person you are. Something that we all could borrow is a bad start.

Off to a Better Start

Believe that you can't possibly compete with your brother's flawless academic achievements. Grimace when he receives an SAT score of 2260. Spend at least four hours a night on homework; observe as your brother seems to finish in minutes. He receives straight A's. Curse angrily when you see him racing around school, his Acceptance Letter clutched in his hand. Interpret the smile on his face as an indication that you can't achieve what he did. Gasp as he lectures the family on the pros and cons of socialism. Be angry knowing that, although you try much harder, he achieves much more ...

Wow ... I wonder where this is going? I want to keep reading. And I already know quite a lot about the author's family and his life as the younger brother. I can't predict if this essay will soar or crash, but so far it has engaged me and told me something substantive about this student, this family, this life.

Drafting

If you have followed the steps in Chapter 4, you are now in the midst of drafting. You have a list of characteristics and an idea or two about what you want the college to know about you; you also have an idea bank to draw from for evidence of your curiosity or your love of young children or your long-standing interest in math and science. And you have chosen a lens, a question from the Common Application's options through which to show your reader this interesting facet of your personality. You've narrated the experience or described the place or the issue, and you have connected that to your theme. Don't worry about having a fabulous introduction. You don't need that. Just get to the heart of the matter, the event or the decision or the failure, and save space for your reflections and insights about it. If you get a half-screen of text down and can't proceed, can't add anything even after giving it a day to percolate, then move on to another of your ideas. There are resources in your bank. You can't be "stuck" for an answer. The critical criteria are, as with every essay, the *claim* and the *proof*. Be sure you have something to say that isn't clear from the rest of your application. And be sure your evidence is specific and complete.

A First Effort

A significant event in my high school career has been my involvement in many activities outside of academics. Working with my peers in musicals, tennis, dance class, volunteer work and various committee and staff work, I have gained a sense of achievement and accomplishment. I have learned to work better with people, learning the value of team effort. I have gained an appreciation for the talent and hard work contributed by each and every person concerned with the project. Working in Maine during the past few summers, I have learned much about dealing with people in a great variety of situations. My co-employees, being older than I am, also helped me to mature and accept things as they are. Furthermore, I now know more about the economic aspect of life, both business and personal.

Alas, this is the kind of writing admissions personnel read all day long. It is not, however, the kind of essay they remember, nor the kind that sends a "gray zone" application to the committee for reconsideration. At a highly competitive school, it's the kind of essay that might be classified DOA (dead on arrival). Most important of all, this is not the kind of essay you are going to submit.

A lot of college essays are lazy. This one certainly is. It's not doing much work for the author. "Lazy essays" fail on one of two counts. Many are too general and can apply to any applicant ("I have learned to work better with people, learning the value of team effort …"). This essay fails because it is unfocused; it could be used by almost any high school senior. Okay, you didn't summer in Maine. Make that California or any place in between. And you were more interested in lacrosse and the yearbook than tennis, dance and the school musicals. Two changes. Whatever else this response has going for it, it can't do much for the author if two changes could make it yours. It wastes the opportunity to convey to the admission committee a fresh and vital sense of the writer. Bill Hiss, at Bates, calls these "Boy Scout" essays. They describe an ideal student — eager, involved, loyal, thrifty, reverent — but it's a general picture, not a real person.

The other way an essay can be lazy is in its unsubstantiated claims ("I now know more about the economic aspect of life…."). While the overly general essay is a generic and forgettable autobiography or travelogue, the passionate essay without evidence is unconvincing. If your summer trip to Colorado taught you to respect nature, there better be five to six actions you've undertaken since your return (the tree planting project at school, the recycling bins you set up, your single-handed effort last January to get the family to tolerate a home thermostat set at 60 degrees) that prove it's so. (BTW, are any of your siblings still speaking to you?)

Regardless of your topic, make your essay show up and shout "Pick me!" Be sure you have a sharp and personal focus, a claim about yourself worth presenting, and the evidence, the stories, and the details to convince your reader that you have, in fact, respected nature or learned that hypotheses are sometimes disproven, or that you reconciled yourself to living with a brother whose accomplishments seem greater than yours (when they're probably just different).

Revising for Specifics

Here's an example of a short piece about a job experience. The claim is reasonable. The author managed to wangle a part-time summer fill-in job through a family connection and discovered there was another side to urban living he'd not seen before. His insights show an observant and reflective habit of mind:

Example 1

The job I had this past summer expanded my level of maturity and provided me with exposure to a world that I had not previously experienced. It involved a combination of a job as doorman and a custodial worker in a New York apartment building. This job allowed me to break out of my shell and see the spectrum of the world as a whole. I have learned balance and adaptability. And I can empathize with the hard-working people of the so-called working class for some of them are now my friends.

But the paragraph seems naïve and lacks the kind of specifics that add credibility and prove his careful observation. It says "Yawn." With some revision, meant to strengthen the evidence, the sample below is starting to do some useful work and starting to say "Pick me!"

Example 2

The job I had this past summer introduced me to physical labor and some new attitudes. I worked a forty-hour week as a doorman and custodian at the Renoir, an apartment building with 120 units on East 78th Street in Manhattan. I had a black tuxedo with a striped vest for half my day and, for the rest of the day, a paint-spattered blue and white jumpsuit that said 'Howie' on the pocket. In either outfit, I often found I was ignored by the people I helped. I got a little more acknowledgment in the tuxedo. I never got a 'Hello' but I did get a few 'Thank you's' from the people I held the door for. As the custodian, I was invisible. I could go four or five hours without hearing a single word directly addressed to me. From this job, I think I learned something about New York, about furnaces, and about the human temperament when deprived of air conditioning. But I also learned something about how our society treats people who do manual labor.

A Complete Essay Sample

Don't expect to nail your essay in the first effort (unless you like to ruminate on topics for weeks before you touch a keyboard). Be satisfied with getting to 800 words and then cut to make those words vivid, memorable and specific. Here's an example (second draft) by an applicant who had an "ah-ha" experience in her high school science class and set out to show her curiosity in an essay about a biology experiment:

Someday, I hope to have a career in the biological sciences. I've always enjoyed the study of science, with its plausible explanations for the 'hows' and 'whys' of our lives. My serious interest in the area of the sciences developed in my sophomore year, when I took Advanced Placement Biology. The final project was designing, conducting and writing up my own experiment.

Although the work involved was time-consuming, doing the experiment allowed me to see how real scientists test hypotheses. My laboratory dealt with the effects of photoperiod and temperature on the growth of *zea mays* seedlings. Not only did I have to care for and daily alter the photoperiods of the plants, I also had to measure, every other day, the heights of 76 corn seedlings. As the labs were to be researched and prepared on a college level, I spent several hours in the library at Washington University and Meramec College, searching the Biological Abstracts to find information on experiments similar to my own which had been written up in scientific journals. The effort required by the lab really made me appreciate the scientists who spend their lives proving or disproving theories by experimentation and research.

Ironically, the experiment was personally rewarding because my original theory was actually disproved. I hypothesized that the plants with the longest photoperiod would grow the fastest. After I concluded the lab and began analyzing the data, however, I found that the plants with a median photoperiod grew faster. I thought that this was very exciting; potentially routine results were given a twist.

I consider my biology experiment to be a valuable scientific experience; I was exposed to the methods and materials of bona fide scientists and, in a small way, felt the excitement of discovery. That laboratory intensified my interest in science. Last year, in chemistry, I conducted more self-designed experiments, including one to test the amount of copper in copper chloride, and another to determine the amount of oxygen required for survival by a fish, a mussel and a clam. These experiments were also worthwhile, but I still consider the zea mays experiment to be the most exciting lab I've ever done.

Nice work by the author and by the essay. Is this Pulitzer Prize reporting? No. Could a little editing tighten it up? Yes. But a sense of this girl — her way of looking at the world, her involvement and enthusiasm — comes across. And unless you took Advanced Placement Biology, did a corn experiment, researched the Biological Abstracts database, practiced scientific research, and made connections between your work in that class, other classes and your career plans, you couldn't submit this particular essay. Its strengths are its clear focus (the Advanced Placement experiment) and its specifics (the class, the 76 seedlings, Biological Abstracts, Meramec, copper chloride, the clam). These make it memorable and uniquely hers. "Students need to unpack their own interests," advises Curtis Rodgers at Columbia. This essay does that. The *claim* and *proof* are what do the job. The writer shows her points. She says she enjoyed the study of science and the 76 seedlings prove it.

What's Left to Do?

Once you have a reasonable draft of your core essay, make a list of all the other questions you need to answer. In the Writing Supplements, there may be additional essays. There will doubtless be a handful of "Why in particular do you wish to attend [College X]?" in the required supplements. Create a document which lists all the additional writing you need to complete, along with the name of the school, its deadline and word limits. Then look for ways to minimize the pain and capitalize on overlap. An answer asking you to describe your family can easily be reworked for a question about how and where you grew up. An answer about an important intellectual experience can legitimately be used to account for an area of academic interest.

Revisit the material in your idea bank when you need to start from scratch. And don't force or wrench a good family essay about your little brother into a bad essay about your hero. With a little planning and consolidation, however, your "What's Left" list should have only four to five items on it.

The Master List

Here's a sample of a master list for our applicant interested in science study:

Schools:	Duke, University of California Santa Barbara, Washington University, Carnegie Mellon, Wellesley, University of Michigan
Core essay:	Claim — my inquiring style Lens — my *zea mays* seedlings experience
Supplements:	1. Important extracurricular activity/accomplishment (optional for Duke, UCSB, UMichigan): soccer
	2. Why us? (UMichigan, Carnegie Mellon, Wellesley)
	3. A book that had an impact on me (Carnegie Mellon): *Guns, Germs and Steel* by Jared Diamond
	4. A community I'm part of (UCSB, UMichigan): my family

5. The diversity of my experience (optional for Duke): maybe — I'm still thinking about this one

6. Note to self: no supplement for Washington University

By creating this list, you will have a good sense of all that's required. (By posting it on your bedroom door, you will have parents with lower blood pressure and an improved sense of control.) Here, the applicant has settled her focus — "my inquiring style" — as well as the lens through which this will be seen. She has soccer for her extracurricular involvement and her growth there might be sufficient for UCSB's request for an essay about an accomplishment. She will have to create a "Why Us" paragraph and populate it with information about three different schools. Not overwhelming as she has a good idea of her areas of interest and has chosen a set of schools that all offer exceptional science facilities. She has visited and carefully researched her schools with a set of "must have" features in mind. She will have to write two additional short pieces, one just a single sentence about a book that has had an impact on her and one about a community she is a part of (to be used for both UCSB and for University of Michigan). She needs to be careful not to replicate her core essay there, so "a community of scientists" might not be the right choice. Something personal might enrich these applications, so family is a good choice.

What else? She has the option to write about the diversity of her experience for Duke and perhaps the thinking that goes into her family essay could be put to use there. Or she may have a unique perspective to relate. But it's optional. They mean that. It doesn't mean you are supposed to have such a perspective; it just means that if you have, they'd like to hear about it. (Another applicant might have used that experience already as a story "central" to his identity. He might skip this question, too.) Just because there's a space, you don't necessarily need to put something in it.

As you can see here, careful planning can uncover overlap and keep additional writing to a minimum. The outliers here are a book selection, the optional diversity essay, and the request for a reflection on community. Not too overwhelming and the idea bank is there as a guide.

Remember that colleges rethink and revise their supplement questions often, hoping to broaden the range of responses and reduce the number of predictable or "safe" essays they receive. A question about a miracle you witnessed, a moment when your perspective changed, a dream job or your own personal theme song is meant to draw forth highly personal and therefore differentiating responses. So let that request for your favorite book be fun!

The Activity Question

Colleges have, for years, asked students to expand on or reflect on an involvement, in or outside of school. It doesn't have to be football captain or a summer on an underwater archeological exploration off the coast of Sicily. A club, a fund-raiser, a team, your church group, your part-time job, or puttering around in the kitchen on big holidays are possible topics if you devote significant time to one of these, find important insights there, or have perhaps taken on a leadership role.

Be sure the function of the group is clear—is *The Mirror* the yearbook or the newspaper?—and elaborate on your role—"recruited 22 new members" is better than "increased participation." As one admission staffer put it, "At some schools the Spanish Club is just a bunch of kids who get together on Friday nights for tacos." Choose an activity where you've put in significant time and had a quantifiable impact.

One other point to consider. You might want to settle this answer's topic before you absolutely commit to the lens or claim of your core essay. If you're all about the local food bank or the tennis team, decide if that's better in an activity supplement or more reflective of your creativity, compassion, or commitment in the core essay. If it is, in fact, "central to your identity" or a place you are "perfectly comfortable," use it for your main essay. Plan ahead.

Off to a Good Start

I am president of the Book Worms, a school club that does volunteer work for the town library. Each month I attend meetings with the library staff and schedule time slots and assignments for other club members; I also work at the reference desk.

Off to a Better Start

As president of my school's Book Worms club, I attend a monthly 2-hour planning meeting at the town library, assign afternoons/evenings to 11 volunteers, and on Tuesday from 7–9pm shelve, scan, answer questions and reboot computers.

Shorter, better, more specific. Plenty of room to take us to the reference desk and show us why you run this little group. And if they've asked for only 200 characters, you're done!

But be aware that admission offices have a pretty good idea of how much free time high school students *don't* have these days. Don't oversell an activity. The student who founded the Animal Rights Club in May of his junior year and is now president is clearly not so much interested in animal rights as in nice-looking credentials on his application. Be clear and — above all — honest.

Lists

The Common Application asks for a list of principal activities. Space is provided to list honors and distinctions as well as your intentions about continuing this activity in college. Other applications ask for other lists or grids: what you've been reading, what you do for fun, best movie of all time. Completing these answers shouldn't require soul-searching agony over the "right" answer, misleading enhancement of the time involved, or any effort to guess what they want you to say. You'll need to think a little, limit yourself to the genuine truth, and show a judicious sense of selection. They're more likely to believe you loved *Gone Girl* than *The Mill on the Floss*.

The "Why Us?" Question

"What aspects of Santa Clara make it one of your top choices?"

"Why NYU?"

"Briefly discuss your reasons for applying to Colby."

Consolidation and looking for overlap works everywhere except for the "Why us?" questions. These you cannot recycle. These responses must be highly individualized and specific. The format for answering each one may be similar: your academic reasons, followed by your other reasons. But what you saw when you visited is unique. What you want to do there will be shaped by their offerings. The programs and features of every school are their distinctions and their pride. Only what they offer and how you plan to exploit those offerings demonstrate genuine and convincing interest.

The "Why Us?" question is actually one of the oldest essay questions because it gets right to the heart of the matter. You have to have done your homework, both the looking in for who you are and what you want, and the looking out to see where four years of meaningful learning are to be found. The college wants to know you have a plan and won't just curl up in your room and sleep until 1 p.m. now that Mom isn't there to pull you out of bed. And they need to be sure they can give you the experiences you are seeking. One of my own children, as we were driving him down the New Jersey Turnpike headed for first-year orientation, suddenly sat up from the handbook he was reviewing and said, "Wait! They don't have a football team?!?!" Make sure you know what you want; make sure the schools you are considering can deliver.

The focus and the proof for "Why Us?" questions are obvious: The focus is the connection between you and the school, the proof is on the campus. Review the pluses of the school and how you came to choose it. Do more research. Read newer postings on their website, look at your college visit journal, ask a recent alumni (the ideal selection would be a recent graduate of your own high school), talk to your school counselor; confirm that your "must haves" are offered. From this you can focus on the main connection between you and the school.

Begin with the more significant factors — curriculum offerings, class settings (tutorials, conferences, lectures), majors, special programs, facilities, locations (if that's important for your studies rather than for your social life). Then move to lesser points — social features, climate, housing options, school traditions, clubs, the vegan snack bar.

If you're fairly sure of your career goal or major area of study, make that your thesis; then show what the school has to offer in your particular concentration. But again, be sure they do have what you need and want. This is as important for you as it is for them. Is the faculty first rate? (Ask friends or teachers about the faculty roster.) Are there some well-known people in your chosen field teaching there? Does the library have a unique section devoted to American political science, Judaica, the letters of W.E.B. DuBois? Cite specific factors that tie in with your primary interest. For example, if you plan to concentrate in international relations at NYU, you might write about the Global Liberal Studies curriculum, the intensive language study program, the campus in Shanghai, the United Nations document depository at Bobst Library, and the autumn internship fairs (human rights activism, research in U. N. peacekeeping force effectiveness) sponsored by the Wasserman Center.

Don't try to flatter the admissions reader with assertions about "world-class faculty," "rich diversity," or the number of books in the library. Instead, make clear a solid knowledge of your own interest and the related advantages of the particular school and its programs.

> I want to work in the health care field. But how I want to do this is still not perfectly clear to me. That's why Georgetown's nursing and health studies school appeals to me. I want the breadth of a B.S.N., rather than just an R.N., perhaps combined with coursework in biology. And I don't want to feel sectioned off and "different" from the rest of the school's undergraduate body. So I like the idea of mixed undergraduate housing. Washington's hospitals offer opportunities for practical experience and the size of the program means I won't get lost. The nursing/pre-medical option also seems right for me since I am still considering medical school.

Your answer, whether 100 words or a full essay, should show your interest and prove the school's "fit" with you. Dig in, find out, and then use your knowledge. And don't use the phrase "I fell in love." This isn't about passion — it's about a reasoned and careful selection process.

"Why Us?" Plus

"Assess your reasons for wanting to attend [College X]. How have your previous experiences influenced your current academic and/or career plans?"

Note here the two parts of this question. Both something about your past and something about your future should be a part of your answer here. Double questions also show up when you are asked "What attracted you to [College X] and what will you contribute to our community?" Find connections between the college and your strengths and interests. Then decide what percentage of the answer ought to treat the school and what percentage ought to treat you. This may be a chance to follow the advice about conclusions in Chapter 3. You can devote most of the answer to your area of interest and use the conclusion as a springboard for a further idea — here, to make a connection to the college or to suggest where you might get involved or what role you might take in the activities or the department of your choice. Remember, however, to sort out how much attention each of the two requests deserves. And be specific.

A Word About Length

Once you've sketched out what you have to do, you can see that your answers will vary in length. Some questions provide a word count, others a character (with spaces) limit. Draft about 50 percent more than the word limit; then edit to the space provided. Read Sample 10 in Chapter 8 to see how one topic can serve for a full-length essay or be edited to a short, tight paragraph. The college is suggesting how extensive and complex an answer they want by the parameters they supply. Let that be your guideline. Don't fall too short or go beyond the limit. Admissions readers are assigned many folders to evaluate and are not perusing your application at their leisure. Make your answers a shot of espresso, not a pot of tea.

Summary

1. Many essays = one essay: "Tell us about yourself."

2. Your audience is a group of seasoned admission professionals who have long experience reading student essays. Don't try to write an essay on a subject they've never read about before — because they have, in fact, seen and read it all. They are not university faculty, for the most part. This means they are interested in you as a person and as a student; they do not expect your essays to be miniature doctoral dissertations or to use the word "inauspicious."

3. The motive of your essay is "Pick me!" You are about to undertake the pleasure of "pitching" yourself to a ready and interested audience. If there is a hard part at all to this, it is only in the choosing of the right lens. Advocate for yourself. What do they need to know about you? Now make your essay *work* for you.

Toolbox: The High-Risk Essay

"I'm applying to a school with 35,000 applicants that enrolls 1,600. My application seems to fit the profile on their website, and last year one of the seniors with something like my credentials was admitted. My guidance counselor says he's 'guardedly optimistic.' Should I go for a big impact on my essay? Could that get me in? I need something!"

The essay is important, but no single aspect of the application can get you into a college. The essay can make a difference, but it is not sensible to believe that a knockout essay will get you into a school when many other factors are shouting "LONG SHOT." Don't try to do something that will "make up for all the rest" of your application — it will only lead to embarrassment and disappointment.

Okay, you *are* a qualified applicant for this school, but you need to stand out. You've decided you want to be different. You've had it with "safe" and decided you want to write an essay that is a "powerful tipper" for your case. Can it be done? Maybe.

Think of the Academy Awards. Dozens of people make similar acceptance speeches that night. What makes any of them stand out in our memories?

1. *Surprise* does. Some acceptance speeches say things we aren't expecting to hear. You could write about a point from your self-outline that few other writers would choose. For example, instead of writing about your concern for children, you could write that procrastination essay.

2. *Form* can do it. Some speakers surprise us not with what they say but with how they say it. A narrative essay may have enough suspense (if it isn't too long) to give this added element. The student who described a 250-toothpick bridge that supported 286 pounds and won him a physics competition made it real by sending the bridge along. Neither event was the basis for acceptance but both were memorable. But think long and hard about going in this direction. Post a YouTube or website link if it really is something individual, of very high quality, and related to the total impact of your application. The toothpick bridge would not have enhanced the application if seven others were sent, if it had supported only eight pounds, or if the applicant wanted to become a music major. Research the admission committee a little before you send anything. If faculty is involved, tapes, artwork and projects may get attention. But remember the volume of applications that have to be reviewed; don't expect more than your share of attention. Nonrequired support materials on a CD may not be reviewed for reasons of time and accessibility. Place

a link in Additional Information or through SlideRoom if the link is enabled as part of an arts supplement — but only if the material is of superior quality and essential to understanding your application. Remember your reader. "I guess I can tell if it's really, really bad," says Jennifer Fondiller at Barnard with a laugh, "but I'm not an artist — pictures of your paintings would strengthen an application to art school, but they're not forwarded to the art department here."

3. The *unusual* can grab lagging attention. Special circumstances — and I mean really special — can make a distinctive essay. "I didn't realize that my mother was deaf until I was in first grade; signing came with speaking for me and transactions between the deaf world and the hearing world were a matter of course. Play dates were where the complications set in. ..." But be careful. You can't borrow someone else's experience or suggest that what they've accomplished belongs to you.

4. *Humor* usually works — *real* humor. A lot of high school humor is goofy, embarrassing, or in poor taste. Just remember Noel Coward's advice: "Wit ought to be a glorious treat, like caviar. Never spread it about like marmalade." Get a second (and a third) opinion, especially of a YouTube or video clip.

5. And, of course, *shock* can do the job ... either for or against you. You want to be clever not silly, a risk taker, not a fool. John Bunnell, associate dean and director of admission emeritus at Stanford, cautions, "The problem is there's a thin line between being humorous and being flip, between being creative and being eccentric. Taking risks is not a negative quality, but there ought to be some common sense involved." Applicants who, given one day in time to spend with anyone in history, choose Britney Spears haven't thought much about their options. A YouTube submission should be the result of as much reflection, consideration, and restraint as any written work you submit. And please don't write about your first sexual experience.

You have to weigh the risk. Of course, there is often a high reward where there is a high risk. Cleopatra had herself delivered to Julius Caesar rolled up in a carpet. That self-presentation worked ... for awhile. Clearly, it takes something special to get a reader to say, "Hey, Alice, listen to this one!" But honesty and your real voice might be memorable enough. While I am sure in the final hours of committee meetings on "gray zone" applications, no one has ever said, "Hey, wait a minute, what about that kid who wrote the essay about a community service project?" I also know that "Listen to this one!" isn't always said about essays that worked. A predictable essay doesn't damn its author as much as a tasteless attempt to astonish and surprise. Take a chance if that's your nature. You may find a like-minded individual on the committee who champions your application because of your essay. Whatever you write should be specific. And do get a couple of opinions on it; long hours at a desk can blur your sense of right versus ridiculous.

Chapter 6

A Family Affair

Going to college is a family affair. The student is the main character, but all the family members — and all the family finances — take a supporting role. Parents advise, assist, and begin to imagine a smaller household. Siblings enjoy the shift of attention but also miss the older (and wiser?) brother or sister. Everyone says, "Thank goodness for FaceTime." And the dog wonders why no one is sleeping in Junior's bed.

College selection, then, is collaboration. And it is probably the first family collaboration in which the child has a greater say than the parents. This chapter, therefore, offers some advice to parents as their children complete applications and write essays. It is meant to normalize the shocks and surprises, challenges and changes of this complicated and exciting moment. And although the rest of this book makes clear what role the applicant needs to take, this chapter addresses assignments for parents and guardians, *particularly assignments related to essay-writing time.* Parents, regardless of their own educational experiences, can provide significant support for their children when it comes time to "Tell us about yourself."

Research I conducted for the National Association for College Admission Counseling asked seniors about their essay composition processes. The range of resources students turned to for help surprised me. Nearly every respondent acknowledged some kind of assistance in the process. But the school counselor didn't rank first. *Parents were the most significant source of help.* Even students living away at boarding schools said their parents helped them at essay time. Teachers, especially English teachers, were cited, as were school counselors, educational consultants, and friends. And of course there has been a proliferation of "help" available on the Web. But the results suggested that parents, who know the lives and personalities of their children, can help a son or daughter think about the topics and sift through their options. All good writers seek feedback, advice, or editing. Yale advises: "Share your essays with at least one or two people who know you well ... and ask for feedback." Parents are uniquely situated to offer this kind of help. Yale continues: "Remember that you ultimately have control over your essays ... but others may be able to catch mistakes that you missed and help suggest areas to cut if you are over the word limit." So feel free to be involved early for ideas and late for proofreading, but leave the topic and the writing to your son or daughter.

A Process for Parents

In the college search, parents and their children talk, reflect, share, think, argue, and come to terms with change. "It's like playing chess naked in a public park," says one veteran parent. "It's not the game you envisioned, not entirely under your control, and way too public to be enjoyable." But remember there's value in the game itself, in the process, as well as in the outcome. So a good first step, before any writing or talking begins, is to look into your own life and consider your expectations and assumptions. The Rev. Zina Jacque, experienced in admission at the University of Chicago, Northwestern, UCSC, and Mills College (she's now the minister of the Community Church of Barrington, Illinois), notes: "Kids pretty consistently apply to at least two colleges: the one their parents went to and the one their parents were rejected by." Whether you went to college or not, you have hopes for your children and, in particular, hopes that they will be even more successful than you are. So consider what you want for your child, separate that from what you want for yourself, and adjust your goals according to what's best for your son or daughter as a learner, as a young adult, "as is."

Timing

The calendar for parents mimics the one provided for students in Chapter 1. The junior year is a time of talk and gentle exploration. Conversations about options and reflections on your child as a learner are useful. There will be some testing that year and a little deflected stress as senior friends go through the search. But it's too early to set the sights or to eliminate anything; so much is still to be determined (grades, scores, captain of debate? conference champs?). For the same reasons, it's a little early to start writing ... but not too early to start banking ideas (see Chapter 5).

In the spring, visit a few campuses as your junior begins to receive school emails. Encourage your son or daughter to take lots of notes. This is the time to make clear that the search needs to be careful, thorough, and in-depth ... not just about reputation, a decal or the stadium. As this year's seniors begin to settle their plans and school counselors focus on juniors, junior-year English teachers may encourage a bit of application-essay drafting or an essay portfolio. A start in May or June can make summer drafting easier. You'll want something in hand by the end of August even if you make revisions when school reopens and counselor or teacher advice is available.

Senior fall is the time of focus — a list of colleges is finalized, with help from the school counselor, and applications are completed — usually one in October if Early Decision is the plan, two if an Early Action school is on the list, and the rest before the winter recess. Be sure your son or daughter has completed all the materials necessary to apply to their full list before they receive their Early Decision results. Waiting to hear from A before you prepare B through G is a dangerous gamble. And remember, the high school will be closed in the days leading up to the first of the year, so be sure all your emergencies happen before the classrooms and offices close.

Winter, as for bears, is for hibernation. Another flurry of activity comes with early spring. Students hear from the colleges in March and April and choose by May 1. There will be confusions, delights, and disappointments. Ideally, several colleges your senior chose will choose her. The summer will include one trip to a giant store called something like Bed, Bath and Futon, and then several moments designed to make home a place she's willing to leave. ("Well, okay, but remember two months from now I'll be able to stay out all night if I want to." "While you're living in our house, young lady ..." You get the idea.) Then they're gone, and it's very quiet. This is a new phase, the right next thing, something you've worked for: less laundry, more email, joy, confusion, adventure, change. You will remember that Mark Twain wasn't kidding when he said, "Youth is wasted on the young."

What You Can't Do

Before the "to-do" list, let's consider the "can't-do" list. Perhaps it will be liberating to consider what's not in your control and what's not expected of you.

- You can't make the high school guidance office into your own personal support system. Guidance is happy to help you ... and all the other senior families. If you do receive a significant amount of assistance, thank-you notes (or a plant for the guidance secretary) are appropriate. Teachers who write recommendations also prefer plenty of lead-time and a follow-up thank you.

- You can't take the standardized tests or write your child's essay. Sharpened pencils, an apple, and new batteries for the calculator on test day are the limits of your power. (Tips on the right level of intervention at essay-writing time follow.)

- You can't change your child's decision style or fully protect him from the bumps and abrasions of this very public sorting. Someone will seem to do better without clear merit. Someone will say something cruel. Rejection is never easy. And Susan Kastner Tree, director of college counseling at the Westtown School in Pennsylvania, advises, "The process, done correctly, will have rejection in it somewhere."

- You can't let inertia teach its lesson here. It's easy to say, "Well, if he doesn't get his act together, he'll learn there won't be any choices left." Great for prom tickets or graduation gowns, but not appropriate for the college selection process. Kids are already conflicted and confused about this moment of judgment. They want to leave and they want to stay. They love you and they need to leave. As Diane Anci, dean of admission at Mount Holyoke, says, "They feel like a twig in the river. They ought to be the river." So don't complicate the matter by letting their irresponsibility bring them down. Let life do that later. Be helpful, inspire action, and get to the end as friends.

What You Can Do

You can frame conversations about college selection and the essay. Choose times when no one can distract them — in the car or at McDonalds works sometimes. Ask them to think about themselves as learners. *What classes have they loved? Hated? What teacher was a favorite? A nemesis? Do they like to talk in class? Do they work if no one's checking? Shine in essays and tests, or in comments and arguments in class? In college, will they still want to act, play the violin, pitch fastballs, or run a model United Nations? A bunch of roommates or a single room? Big classes? Group work? Lectures? Vegan menu options? An adjacent city or a remote, silent wilderness? A semester in Shanghai or a summer on an archeological dig?* By talking about the options in the future and the educational experiences in the past, you can help your senior look beyond name brands and think about the match of themselves and specific institutions. In this way, together, you begin building a prototype, i.e., a generic, ideal college template that can be plugged in at a variety of levels of competitiveness and selectivity.

Here's an example: I conclude that I am happiest in small, seminar classes and that the restrictions of a core curriculum are less appealing to me than the ability to choose courses according to my own interests. I am looking into environmental science, but I want a school where I can create my own major in the intersection of this discipline and government policy. I want a coed school, and I don't want fraternities to drive the social scene. I want my teachers to know me and the campus to be four to five blocks, not a ZIP code of its own. I don't want to be more than a three- to four-hour drive or a nonstop flight from home. Now, I can generate a list of six to eight schools (nationwide, there are 3,000 + schools to choose among) that fit the criteria but represent a range of selectivity from the very selective (less than 20 percent of applicants are admitted), through selective (20 percent to 40 percent are admitted), to less selective (greater than 40 percent are admitted). If I can create a clear definition of my perfect school and if all my applications go to schools that fit the prototype, I will get what I want wherever I enroll. (As the parent and chief financial officer in this collaboration, remember to identify any absolutes in the process — if it can't be on the other side of the country or cost more than $20,000, say so early.)

Talking About the Essay

"We all talked about it at the dinner table. Everyone had ideas. Marie, my sister, had this idea ... my Mom helped me, too," says Claire Garpestad, a Wellesley High School graduate now at Washington University. Family can be a powerful resource as a senior starts to think about college and about the application essays. But the emphasis here is on the word "start." In the early stages of thinking, planning, and wondering about an essay topic, family conversations, as long as they are exploratory and not prescriptive, can be useful. You are not a guidance counselor and you haven't read a few hundred application essays every year for the last decade. So don't tell your senior what to write about. *In fact, don't even discuss the essay questions themselves.* The essay is meant to be an additional lens on the applicant, a source of information beyond the scores, grades, and activities list. It is included so that colleges can evaluate the applicant's writing ability and also uncover a sense of the applicant's ideas, values, and point of view. The questions all come down to the same thing: "Tell us about yourself." Your role is to help your child look at that "yourself" and decide what's worth telling. You both have 17 years of information to share; you have the maturity of age to temper the process.

So begin with a conversation about your child's strengths and positive attributes. Tell them what you think they're very good at, your favorite personality features, or a habit of thinking or acting you appreciate. Go for adjectives, not nouns. Talk about what you love about them, what others have said, what comes up in teacher conferences or shines forth in their performances, games, kitchen conversations, or family interactions. A list of first-round thoughts might be: hardworking, committed, enthusiastic, optimistic, energetic, smart, cheerful, willing to help. Or maybe your offspring is creative, spontaneous, generous, innovative, individualistic, reflective, sensitive, adaptable. These lists represent two different people — your green-haired daughter? your sweet C+ son? — but each has strengths.

As an adviser, recast discouragement as hope. If they offer, "I don't know what I want to study," you can offer, "That's good … you're clearly interested in everything!" Not only are you supplying a possible focus for the essay; this conversation is much-needed praise and affection at a time when the world seems rather dark and judgmental.

Your son or daughter may be unwilling to play along with this game. If they don't want your input, you can provide a sympathetic listening ear, asking about their plans to date. Best not to ask about what other people are doing — that feels like criticism. If you are afraid they are heading in the wrong direction, find a school counselor, teacher, coach, godmother, or paid educational consultant to join the process. Experienced and credentialed independent educational consultants can be found through the Independent Educational Consultants Association (IECA) in Fairfax, Virginia (www.iecaonline.org) or through the Higher Education Consultants Association (www.hecaonline.org). When a son or daughter refuses help, it is, of course, a sign of emerging independence (this never seems to apply to the ironing or to car insurance payments). But your senior does need someone as a sounding board. It's easy to get off-track answering any high-stakes question; this is not the time to "go it alone" entirely. Conversely, it's also easy to be intimidated and waste the opportunity with something safe, predictable, and utterly forgettable. An English teacher, a coach, a school counselor, or an independent educational consultant can help. Because of their limited experience, friends are a last resort. But "it takes a village to write an essay," says Brad MacGowan, an educational researcher and counselor at Newton North High School in Massachusetts. For MacGowan, every writer needs "reciprocal contact with knowledgeable adults." So if discourse doesn't happen at your dinner table, encourage your senior to find it on the field, in the classroom … somewhere reliable and supportive and informed.

If, however, the conversation leads to notes on the back of a fast-food napkin, you've got your senior started on an idea bank (see Chapter 5 for some models). Look it over together. Eliminate things revealed by the rest of the application. "Smart" may be adequately addressed by the transcript. "Athletic" will be there in the MVP award. "Involved" will be obvious from the activities list. Then ask yourself if there is a major strength or characteristic missing from your child's application. With only the transcript and scores, will admission know about his drive, his humor, his generous spirit, his creativity, his analytic and inquisitive way of thinking? Can the essay fill in the blanks?

Together or separately you might list some events, stories, or "hot spot" moments that make evident the missing characteristic. Be sure to focus on the characteristic, not the event that reveals it. Choose a story tailored to your theme: creativity (as seen through an alternate assignment developed for 10th-grade science) or insight (as seen through the experience of winning/losing a class election) or stamina and loyalty (as seen through the commitment to a consistently defeated field hockey team). The topic should be the creativity, the insight, or the commitment. The wind tunnel, the race for class president, life as a goalie — use these as illuminations of character and personality. Don't start with an event and try to wring meaning from it. Start with a personal "Pick me!" characteristic, and figure out what story will make that clear and vivid.

Rick Rizoli, a seasoned adviser to families at The Rivers School, says, "The student is the captain — everyone else is the crew." Together, you're a team of experts that can bring both positive energy and a sense of good judgment to the planning. But as the parent, please don't dictate a topic. Even if your senior chooses a weak idea to begin with (and this is the normal pattern), since you're planning a list of possibilities here, there will be an idea bank of options to return to if Plan A turns into Plan B. Regardless of your educational background, first language, income, or achievements, you can help in the essay planning.

Batting around ideas and possibilities is fair game for anyone with an interest in the young person ... but once the writing begins, you all belong on the sidelines. Read Chapters 3, 4 and 5 of this book for a fuller sense of how the writer will proceed after your involvement. But leave the red pencil in your desk and stick with "discourse" as the best way to be helpful.

Final Tips

- Schedule time to generate a preliminary idea bank for the essay, brainstorming together in the junior-year spring and again in the summer. This will serve as a useful resource as the business of applying gets serious. And it has extra benefits. Students need to do some self-examination in order to make wise choices in college; this kind of thinking and talking can enrich every aspect of the application, the interview, and the college experience.

- Talk, don't write. Be active when ideas are flying around, but avoid hands-on editing. Once the ideas are out there, the student should own the rest of the writing process. You might proofread for typos. But a teacher or a school counselor may be a more familiar (and less painful) source of gentle suggestion and light editing (grammatical and usage errors, spots of confusion, school-specific jargon). Stick to talking ideas about the drafts. Don't spoil the spontaneity or change the style of the essay. My experience with hands-on parent editing is that it usually turns a good kid essay into a mediocre lawyer essay.

- Be true to your child. Don't encourage your senior to write about an imagined topic meant to please admission personnel. There is no such thing. You cannot predict who will read an application — the dean with 30 years experience (he loves cross-country skiing, murder mysteries with culinary subplots, and syndicated episodes of *M**A*S*H) or the new hire who graduated last May (she loves yoga, Suzanne Collins, and *Girls*). Instead, focus on what admission needs to know about this applicant. Forget "What should I say?" and ask "What don't they know?"

- Don't despair if you aren't a big part of this collaboration at the beginning. Students do care what their parents think, and you will be important in the final decision, even if you're a sideline adviser along the way. Be ready for soul-searching conversations in April as students make their final decisions and discover that they actually have to leave home and attend one of these places.

Conclusion

Regardless of your knowledge of colleges or your own educational achievements, you are an expert on your child. You are therefore an important helper in this collaboration called "applying to college." Together, you and your senior can work out the right degree of involvement for everyone. Tell your senior you won't nag if he will create a checklist of chores and deadlines and post it on the refrigerator door. Together, make the most of help from the high school but remember that your deadlines are everyone else's deadlines. You can get help from admission offices, too (I promise the admission secretary does *not* keep a log in which to note "Parent of Thomas Smith called — asked a silly question"). Recognize those tasks that are entirely your responsibility, like the necessary tax forms for financial aid applications. Most important, provide encouragement and assure your son or daughter that the process, in general, is fair, supported by helpful professionals, and neither the last nor the only decision they will make about their education and their future. If things go wrong, most mistakes can be corrected (transfer? year off? guest semester?).

At essay-writing time, remind students that:

- they've written essays before; they have the necessary writing skills

- they know (and love) this topic: themselves

- the essay isn't the only factor in the admission decision, but if they work hard, it has the potential to be a positive factor

- there are helpers to turn to

- this is a chance to shine if they can write solid prose of memorable insight

Toolbox: Ten Tips from Experienced Parents[1]

1. "Start early. When they see these schools in junior year, it's too late to get that GPA up."

2. "Rely on your school counselor. Guidance has invaluable information. Our school has a 'destination book' with information about past applicants to all the colleges."

3. "Don't rely on your school counselor entirely. The work is really your child's and yours. You can't expect everything from Guidance. Do the homework. Be involved. Be grateful."

4. "Don't listen to other parents. Scary. There is plenty of misinformation out there."

5. "Don't ask a question on the tour. Embarrassing. Let the kids do the asking."

6. "Never say 'safety.' We used IMPOSSIBLE/PROBABLE/LIKELY. That felt better."

7. Visit … maybe multiple times. Our first tour guide wasn't very informed … and it rained. We went back for another visit later in the process and the Admitted Student Day settled it."

8. "Get rejected. I felt sort of cheated that he didn't get at least one rejection letter because isn't that the only way to be sure you've covered the range?"

9. "Do the math. We started early to look at costs, our resources, and what financial aid was available."

10. "Make it work. That's our family motto. It's a good one."

Pamela Reynolds, an educational consultant based in Boston likes to say, "I loved being a mom. I hated being a parent." This is one time, however, when being a parent is more rewarding than the rule-making of the preschool years. Parents are incredibly important to their daughters and sons as the family dynamic changes and children head off to complete their educations. With patience on both sides, the process — and even the essay — can be a successful collaboration.

---

1 Special thanks to Mary Snow and the united parents of St. George's School, Newport, RI, and of Winchester High School, Winchester, MA.

chapter 7

A Different Story

The essay process described in this book is meant to prepare you to write almost any expository prose assignment. And the details of the process offered in Chapters 4 and 5 should help you feel ready to advocate for yourself with an application essay that is correct in form and unique in content. After all, it's about you, and there will be no other essays about you. Just keep on the topic of you, and don't wander off into the land of "what they want to hear." Your focus should be "what they need to know."

The fact that every applicant is unique, however, means that the formulas given in the chapters so far may not quite do the job for you. This chapter is devoted to some of the special circumstances that tax the application essay with doing more than the essay of the average high school senior. But don't be discouraged by difference. Admission offices read applications holistically; where you've been and who you are will be factored into every part of their evaluation. The most obvious example is a nonnative speaker of English; essays in that application will not be held to the same standard applied to the writing of native speakers. The transcript from an applicant from *Collège Lycée International de Ferney-Voltaire* won't be worth more or less because it doesn't match that of a 17-year-old at Central High School in Springfield, Missouri. Every factor builds the context for the applicant's essay — one of the reasons this business isn't done by machines. Embrace your difference and look forward to writing about it in your applications.

If You Are an American Applying to American Colleges from Abroad

Thousands of young people apply to American colleges from schools around the world. In our very global economy, of course, an American high school student can be from Turkey as easily as from Tennessee. But most American ex-pat families, happy to have their children at home through high school, want them to attend American universities. If this is your situation, you have plenty of interesting experiences to relate and perhaps full mastery of a second language. It is tempting, too, to feel a little smug about all this when you reconnect with old friends from elementary school who've never left Winnetka.

American colleges know that international students will diversify their student populations, adding voices from all over the world and from all over the experience map. The same formula mentioned in Chapter 5 should be useful to you: Think about yourself and ask what you might contribute to a group — talents, interests, experiences — that will make the conversations at College X more interesting. Julie Browning, dean of enrollment management at Rice University, explains how she looks at essays: "We take a holistic approach. What are your intellectual passions? What talents and leadership potential do you possess? Will you add to the 'spirited discourse' here?" If your essay can answer these questions, it will help the admission office determine how you might fit into the class. Think about what you hope to do in college and share that; the supplemental questions often offer the right opportunity to explain "what you will add to the community."

And be sure you think about your application in the context of all those that will be received at College X. It may seem unusual to you that you are in school in London or in Hong Kong, but it will not be unusual to your reader. Kristin Dreazen, an independent counselor in London, encourages her advisees to look beyond the obvious red bus on London Bridge to convey who they are. "I encourage them to engage in their community," she suggests, "and not to view living abroad, in and of itself, as a unique distinction."

Experiences imposed on you ("My Dad's job transplanted the whole family to Turin") shouldn't be your topic; the reasons for living in Turin will probably be clear from other parts of the application. Focus on what you've made of the circumstances, how they have made you more knowledgeable, more curious, or open-minded. A first encounter with unfamiliar currency, food, or habits of hygiene isn't going to make a distinctive essay unless you can work it into an interesting and self-revealing "And so." And, as with any large and complex yourself if you try to create an "American high school kid" essay. Experiences that happened to you ("I am one of five brothers" or "My father died when I was three") are successful essay topics only if they can function as a lens on your personality. The same can be said of your cultural heritage. While this might be woven into every part of your application, to a large extent it will be there without your pointing to it or using your core essay to explain that you were born and raised in Guangzhou. Students are admitted to be active members of the classroom experience and not to fulfill a "shopping list" of diversities. Whatever you may have to write about, your national heritage will appear. But don't make that the topic. Make a personal characteristic — your quirky love of geometry, your tenacious efforts to master physics, your time spent with a sibling — the focus. Tara Dowling, a college counselor with experience from Moscow to Shanghai, says, "Don't tell the macro story; tell the micro story."

And if you put your essay out for professional polishing, you will lose all the value of its being a "personal" statement. To prepare yourself for the American educational experience where learning is co-created in the intersection of instruction and conversation, thinking and writing about yourself for a "Tell us about yourself" essay is a valuable endeavor.

If English Is Not Your First or Best Language

Every student is nervous about their writing. But if English is not your first or best language, you will be acutely aware of this. Writing an essay in a language you haven't fully mastered is a challenge. There is a lot of forgiveness in a conversation but words on the page take on a more serious tone. Mistakes jump out and the rules are a bit more strict than in a chat with a bilingual friend. However, while it is tempting to get an editor who will make everything perfect, you don't want to misrepresent your skill level.

Don't write your essay in your native language and then translate it. This seemingly logical strategy rarely produces a readable or vivid result. And resist having a native speaker revise for you. The small stylistic variations are what give your essay texture, a sense of the writer behind the keyboard, the authenticity of a voice. If you wear a mask, you will have to wear it forever. Passing this off to someone else erases who you are. And your essay will be viewed in the context of the rest of your application. Admission readers will discount the essay entirely if its polish exceeds that found in the rest of your credentials and reference letters.

topic, move slowly to the idea of writing about poverty. There is no doubt that privilege is not distributed evenly throughout the world and that there are many places where living conditions are unhealthy or uncomfortable. But what do you want to say about this other than how unfortunate it is? "Don't make it a 'trip to the aquarium' essay," says Scott White, at Morristown High School. "'I went there, I saw the fish, I came home' is only something that happened. Not something you've thought about. And 'It made me so sad; it changed my world forever' isn't much of a thought anyway."

If you follow the scheme in Chapter 5 and begin with a clear sense of a personal characteristic you want the college to learn about, you can find a reasonable story or lens to convey that. But an essay that relies on the fact it takes place in Moscow or Mumbai is not going to help your case.

If You Are an International Student Applying to American Colleges

You will not find advice here about how to research American colleges, testing you need to take, or how to acquire a visa once you are admitted you will find suggestions about how to tailor your writing education a prepare the American college application essays and about how to avoid of the common errors in making your applications.

You may never have written a personal essay before. Plenty of educ systems throughout the world train students in academic writing scholarship and leave the style of the personal memoir out of the curr So you may wonder why an admission office would want to know more your personality, values, family, or reflections. Additionally, your context may not encourage or value personal writing of the kind rec answer a question like "Discuss a 'Why not?' moment in your academic or social life" (Lafayette College) or "Identify and describe a habit or idiosyncrasy — of any nature — that helps define you" (O College). Collectivist cultures value shared points of view and disco even reject) highly individual behaviors and opinions. Writing al family may feel dishonorable. Admission offices will of course take t of factors into account as they read your personal statements.

But if you are going to survive and thrive at an American colle want to work on getting comfortable with the revealing habit th characterize a lot of the American youth culture. You won't

Work on the story first and the English last. Develop your ideas and frame them in a way that makes sense to you. Read your essay out loud to a native speaker for the sake of coherence. But stick with the real thing. Admission likes the real thing. "Great essays get passed around," says Nina Lococo, vice president for enrollment management at Carroll College in Montana, "and they aren't always the most well-written ones. We get excited when we feel we're reading something authentic."

Colleges understand the complexity of the circumstances of ESL and ELL students. They do not use the same standard of judgment on every student. Best to write the way you write. That's what your papers and tests will look like in college. The college knows what additional facilities can be provided and you should, too. Mention the Writing Center or the tutorial programs in your "Why Us?" answers if you feel you will need writing support. But let the essay stand on its own merits.

A Sample from an Applicant in Shanghai

If human being comes from anthropoid's exploring journey from forest to plain, due to its curiosity about the life there, My discovery journey was actually begun with a "super evil crime" when I was 5 years old. One day, by coincidence, I found out my farther's treasured stamp album. "What is on those small pictures?" I was so curious. I simulated my farther to study them. However, the result was most stamps were damaged. But, my farther didn't go outrageous after he got home. He picked up a damaged stamp. It is called "The nine Planets' Party", in memory of a special astronomical event that nine planets in solar system lined up on May 16, 1982. Looking at this small stamp, my farther told me many things about the earth, the solar system and the Galaxy, which opened my mind to the immense cosmic space. My science discovery journey started and philately becomes one of my hobbies.

The style of this essay — and even the occasional spelling error — do not detract from the message. The applicant has made it clear that if she is admitted to an American college, she will bring scientific curiosity and a readable mastery of written English that will improve.

If You Are the First in Your Family to Apply to College

Colleges are committed to broad-based education and hope to bring into their classrooms all kinds of students who will contribute to the conversations there and benefit from the campus opportunities. Whether your parents went to college or not has no bearing on this. Your essay should, like everyone else's essay, reflect your enthusiasm for the institution and uncover personal strengths not evident from the rest of the application. Read Chapters 4 and 5. The advice there applies equally to you. If you don't go home every day to a family well-versed in the college application process and comfortable giving advice about options, interviews, and testing strategies, don't be discouraged. Explore the expertise in the guidance office and capitalize on the goodwill of the teachers who like you. Talk to your parents about your strengths and talents. They know a lot about your interests, commitment, and enthusiasm. Then tell your story. That will be enough.

If You Are Headed Back to School

That life away from school has already begun changes the tone and flavor of any "back to school" application. If you stopped, make a convincing case for why you need to start again. People advance their education at different times and in different ways. You may have been in rehab or you may have been sailing around the world. Things happen, both good and bad. Your application essay is a chance to show what value these experiences, adverse or advantageous, have had for you. Again the colleges are looking for students who are committed and bright but who offer different points of view. Don't overlook the chance to show that whatever has happened to you, it wasn't wasted.

Thus, in this case, the traditional high school senior's application essay about personality and passions is less valuable than a clear articulation of what you've been doing since you left school and why this particular college is the right step for you now.

Be straightforward about failures and forthright about mistakes. Your essay will align with the "Tell us about yourself" concept explored in Chapter 5, but there will be more autobiography —"mental autobiography" — here, the evolution of your life plans. You will, like the transfer, be doing this without the aid of the high school office. Consider hiring an independent educational consultant from IECA (www.iecaonline.com) or HECA (www.hecaonline.org) to guide you. Your essays will advocate for you best if they explain your thought process in high school, your activities since then, your maturation, and, most importantly, exactly what you want from college and where you're going with it.

If You Are a Veteran Applying at the End of Your Service

"Life has happened," says Curtis Rodgers at Columbia University School of General Studies. "A professional dancer, a 30-year-old, a recently discharged Marine, an Olympic fencer: Our applicants have experienced life." Not so different from the 17-year-old's challenge but clearly the experiences are different. Colleges are interested in the leadership skills and life experience of veterans. The essay is the ideal place to talk about these topics. So a veteran making a first application to college should show where she is in her life progression and what she's thought of the journey so far. Rodgers points out that veterans make important contributions to their classes and the conversations found there, especially in mathematics, Middle Eastern studies, and political science classes. It is not necessary to have done miraculous things. Beth Morgan, Director of Higher Education Initiatives for the USMC Leadership Scholar Program, notes: "Our applicants are a welcome diversity on campuses because Marine Corps applications highlight experiences that most people will not have acquired in a lifetime." Serving your country in any capacity is admirable and likely to have produced many opportunities to think about your own character and how you interact with others.

As a veteran you will not have the full battalion of a school counseling office to support your application efforts. You may feel that while you want to go to college, your experiences have drawn you away from, rather than toward, education. *A cappella* competitions, football rallies, and winter streaking may seem only remotely interesting. For you, work is important, not feelings. Some veterans are reluctant tellers, reticent about their experience and unsure what parts relate to being admitted to college. Begin by looking in and then find the story that shines some light on the character or set of values you've discovered there. Choose a characteristic and ask yourself, "When was that evident in my life?" Stories of work, comradeship, or the experience of another culture can advocate for you.

Plan to find some guidance as you prepare your application. Your former high school counselor may be willing to meet and discuss your options. There are advisers within the military system as well. And college admission officers are a wonderful resource. Rodgers travels to military bases to talk to potential students and to encourage the stories from their service. Here again, Chapters 4 and 5 should be helpful to you in guiding your thinking through the events to the personal reflections they have inspired.

If You Are Thinking of Transferring

Almost every first-year student thinks about transferring in the cold, long days of February and March. Even at Florida State and California State Long Beach! If you pursue that thought, don't plan on using the essays you wrote for that first college admission process. The admission office will be most interested in your "journey," how you came to be at a school that is unsatisfactory, what is missing for you there, and how they will be able to offer you a better experience. The reasons should be driven mostly by academic considerations. A clear explanation of your course of study as well as your career plans is appropriate for a transfer essay. You aren't going off to college now with the unformed plans of a high school senior.

Make your essays well-articulated statements of your plans, what you've mastered and what you need to complete to achieve specific career goals. Let your essay tell that story; chronological order might be the best way to construct it. You have an advantage and a disadvantage. Admission will consider you a survivor. You have already "gone to college," a stumbling block for a surprising number of young people. You've moved out, done your own laundry, and survived. All to the good. But admission offices are more tolerant of the undecided and unfocused applicant to a freshman class. So make clear where the growth has occurred and what your plans are. Transfers are expected to be fairly orderly about their future. And the college's reservation will focus on what drove you out of College X. Make sure your reasons are solid, your explanation clear, and your expectations well aligned with your target school. Your college list this second time around will be short and very coherent, driven by what didn't happen in your first enrollment and focused on what you plan to do in your second enrollment and beyond.

A Final Word

Hopefully, you have read all of this book as well as Chapter 7. If not, go back and do that now. Because although it may seem that your situation is unique and that the advice given to the "average kid" doesn't work for you, the truth is that the advice in the earlier chapters is just the thing you need. "Look in," brainstorm yourself, find a focus that you want the college to know, and then choose the lens through which you can show this personal characteristic. Vince Cuseo at Occidental gives the best advice for any of these situations: "It always needs to start with self-awareness." This suggestion will make your essay a strong voice in your application. Think of the assignment as an invitation to introduce yourself and tell your story. It's an opportunity to be heard. Make the most of it. And good luck!

Toolbox: Start Fast

Whatever your story, start with energy and move quickly to the meaning. Read Chapter 4, do a little personal life inventory for that "idea bank," settle on something the college ought to know about you, and get it down on paper. It's normal to draft a lengthy introduction ... sort of like clearing your throat as a way to begin ... but these rarely do much more than belabor your choice of topic. In your second draft, see if you can pick up the pace, eliminate repetitions, and go "deeper rather than wider." And in your final draft, get to the point quickly and you'll have more space to thoroughly unpack the meaning of the incident or issue you've chosen.

First Draft of an Introduction

Three delicious meals a day, and a beautiful house to live in. It amazes me how much I take for granted. I never thought of how other people around the world were living, until I visited the home country of my parents, Bangladesh, in 2012 for the first time. To this day I can still remember how people were starving for food and freezing on the streets. The visit was an experience of a lifetime, and it changed my life forever. My visit to Bangladesh was intertwined with another first experience as well. I had never experienced a death in my family. My uncle, whom I was very close to, passed away that year, and he had asked to be buried back home. It was for this reason that my family had traveled to Bangladesh in the first place. I was hit with two emotional milestones at once: the death of my uncle and the experience of seeing a kind of life I had never witnessed before. ...

First Revision

I never thought of how other people around the world were living until I visited the home country of my parents, Bangladesh, in 2012 for the first time. To this day, I can still remember how people were starving for food and freezing in the streets. My visit to Bangladesh was intertwined with another first experience as well: a death in my family. My uncle, whom I was very close to, passed away that year, and he had asked to be buried back home. It was for this reason that my family had traveled to Bangladesh in the first place. I was hit with two emotional milestones at once: the death of my uncle and the experience of seeing a kind of life I had never witnessed before.

Final Introduction

In 2012, for the first time, I visited the home country of my parents, Bangladesh, to attend the funeral of my uncle who had asked to be buried back home. I experienced there both a death and a life I had never witnessed before ....

[Ok, now tell us all about those events and your thoughts about them.]

Chapter 8

Analyzing Some Drafts

"There is no one standard," says Marlyn E. McGrath, director of admission at Harvard. So no one essay can be presented as perfect or "correct." In fact, no one *question* can be presented as ideal or perfect, either. The questions have and will continue to change. But the underlying question, "Tell us about yourself," will abide. The drafts below, several of which respond to the current Common Application questions, have good points and areas that need improvement. Read them all; then read the comments to see where each author needs to keep working and where he or she has succeeded in setting a standard. All are meant to suggest the breadth of options you have in introducing yourself to a college. Emerson said, "Insist on yourself." If you do, your essay will set its own standard.

Sample 1

"Some students have a background or story that is so central to their identity that they believe their application would be incomplete without it. If this sounds like you, then please share your story." — Common Application Question

> I guess it was inevitable that I'd be on hockey skates at some point in my life, but I did not expect that I'd become an ice hockey official before I even reached high school. But being born into a family of hockey players and figure skaters, it seemed that my destiny had already been decided.
>
> Right from the beginning, my two older brothers and my father strapped me up and threw me onto the ice. I loved it and, in my mind, I was on my way to becoming Wayne Grezky! But my mom had to think

of something fast to drag her little girl away from this sport of ruffians. Enter my first hot pink figure skating dress! That was all it took to launch fifteen years of competitive figure skating. It took a great deal of convincing from my parents that competitive figure skating and ice hockey were really the same thing.

I always had an unsatisfied yearning for ice hockey though. My compromise became refereeing; little did I know that I was beginning an activity that would influence my character and who I am today. When I began, I would only work with my dad and brothers. As I began officiating higher-level games and dealing with more arrogant coaches, I entered a new male-dominated world, a world I had never experienced before. My confidence was shot, and all I wanted to do was get through each game and be able to leave. Sometimes I was even too scared to skate along the teams' benches because I would get upset by what the coaches would yell to me. "Do you have a hot date tonight, ref?" was a typical comment that coaches would spit at me during a game. I was determined not to let them chase me off the ice.

I made the decision to stand up for myself. I never responded rudely to the coaches, but I did not let them walk all over me and destroy my confidence. I started to act and feel more like the 4-year certified Atlantic District Official that I am. There were still a few situations that scared me. One time I called a penalty in a championship game during the third overtime and the team I penalized ended up losing because they got scored on. I knew I had made the right call, even though I was unnerved when I saw the losing teams' parents waiting for me at my locker room. That was an important stepping-stone in my officiating career and in my life.

After four years of refereeing, I still can't say it's easy. Every game hands me something new and I never know what to expect. Now I have the confidence and preparation to deal with the unexpected, on and off the ice. I now also know to take everything with a grain of salt and not let it get to me. I have learned that life is just like being out on the ice; if I am prepared and act with confidence, I will be perceived as confident. If you are going to really know me, you need to know that I am a hockey referee.

Things to Notice About This Essay

- The author tells an interesting story about her experiences as a referee.

- A sense of her personality — determination, flexibility, good humor — comes through in the narration.

- Details like "Do you have a hot date tonight, ref?" make the narration memorable (we'd love to hear more of these kinds of details).

- The essay needs a faster start. The first paragraph (three sentences) says the same thing in both the first and third sentences — and gives away the essay's surprise in the second! A good revision would delete all of paragraph one and start at paragraph two. And that edit would free-up word count for the next suggestion.

- There's too much frame here and not enough picture: lots of high-minded assertions ("destiny," "influence my character," "stepping-stone") but not enough detail, especially about the difficulties of becoming and being a ref.

- The author should "dwell" in the meaning of the experience a little more at the end — "I wonder about ... I also think ... Sometimes I believe ..." Woven through many years of the author's life, this story, if it's central to the author's identity, doesn't mean just one thing — there are more insights and lessons to explore here.

Sample 2

"Describe the unique qualities that attract you to the specific undergraduate College or School to which you are applying ..." — University of Michigan

From the time I was able to realize what a university was, all I heard from my mother's side of the family was about the University of Michigan and the great heritage it has. Many a Saturday afternoon my grandfather would devote to me, by sitting me down in front of the television and reminiscing about the University of Michigan while halftime occurred during a Michigan Wolverines football game. Later, as I grew older and universities took on greater meaning, my mother and uncle, both alumni of the University of Michigan, took me to see their old stomping grounds. From first sight, the university looked frightening because of its size, but with such a large school comes diversity of people and of academic and non-academic events.

In Springfield High School, I have taken both AB and BC Calculus and excelled in biology and chemistry. The school's non-academic clubs such as the Future Physicians and the Pylon, both of which I have belonged to for two years, give me an opportunity to see both the business world and the medical world. These two clubs have given me a greater sense of what these careers may be like. In Future Physicians, I participated in field trips to children's hospitals and also participated in two blood banks. I plan to pursue a degree in biology at Michigan and I am excited about the world-class faculty and cutting-edge facilities.

The past three years of my life have given me greater visions of my future. I see the University of Michigan as holding a large book with many unread chapters and myself as an eager child who has just learned to read. I intend to read and probe into all the chapters. The University of Michigan offers me more than the great reputation of this fine school, but a large student body with diverse likes and dislikes, and many activities, both academic and non-academic, to participate in. With the help of the University of Michigan, I will be successful after college and be able to make a name and place for myself in our society. And I can't wait to wear my own Wolverine blue sweatshirt.

Things to Notice About This Essay

- This essay follows the standard essay organization: an introduction, a body paragraph about curriculum and activities, and a conclusion that returns to the idea of Michigan's diversity.

- Nearly everything described here appears elsewhere on the application, under extracurricular activities or alumni connections.

- What's Pylon?

- There are many generalizations but no specific development of these points ("participated" is a pretty vague word). How did his activities give him "a greater sense of what these careers may be like"? The limit is 500 words. There is no pressure to hit that number but even if he sticks with 350, his answer needs to be more specific and informed.

- There is little specific knowledge of the University of Michigan. Has his uncle told him why there are 109,901 seats in Michigan Stadium? "Diversity," "world-class faculty" and "cutting edge facilities" don't add much when the Taubman building, President Gerald Ford, and the crew of Apollo 15 might be mentioned. Colleges ask this type of question to be sure the applicant knows the school and is prepared to take advantage of its offerings.

- A lot of word count is wasted on a long metaphor about a book and its chapters. That needs to go.

- The writer would be well advised to think a bit more about why he is applying to Michigan (family pressure?) and what he will do there … besides buy a sweatshirt. With some serious cutting of the introduction, conclusion, and book metaphor, there will be plenty of word count to discuss the details of life as a biology major at Michigan.

Sample 3

"Reflect on a time when you challenged a belief or idea. What prompted you to act? Would you make the same decision again?" — Common Application Question

My preferred companions are books or music or pen and paper. I have only a small circle of close friends, few of whom get along together. They could easily be counted "misfits." To be plain, I found it quite easy to doubt my ability to have any sort of "close relationship."

After the closing festivities of Andover Summer School this past summer, on the night before we were scheduled to leave, a girl I had met during the program's course came to my room, sat down on my bed, and announced that she was debating with herself whether she wanted me to become her boyfriend. She wanted my reaction, my opinion.

I instantly said, "No." I told her I on no account wanted this and that I would reject any gestures she made towards starting a relationship.

I would ignore her entirely, if need be. I explained that I was a coward. I wanted nothing whatsoever to do with a relationship. I talked a lot and very fast.

To my surprise, she did not leave instantly. Instead, she hugged her knees and rocked back and forth on my bed. I watched her from across the room. She rocked, and I watched. Doubts crept up on me. Opportunity had knocked and the door was still locked. It might soon depart.

"I lied," I said. "I was afraid of what might happen if we became involved. But it's better to take the chance than to be afraid."

She told me she knew I had lied. I had made her realize, though, how much she actually wanted me to be her boyfriend. We decided to keep up a relationship after Andover.

Even then, I was not sure which had been the lie. Now I think that everything I said may have been true when I said it. But I'm still not sure.

I learned, that night, that I could be close to someone. I also realize, now, that it doesn't matter whether or not that person is a misfit; the only important thing is the connection. As long as there is something between two people—friendship, love, shared interests, whatever else—it is a sign that there can be some reconciliation with anxiety, some "fit" for misfits. And it shows that fear need not always win, that we can grow and change, and even have second chances. She was brave; I was surprised. We've continued in that way. I am still seeing her.

Things to Notice About This Essay

- The essay is about a tiny personal challenge, not a national crisis or even a memorable protest; he challenged his own comfort, his own fears. Small can be as good as large.

- It follows the standard essay pattern: an introduction (short), a series of supporting paragraphs for the story of this person's effect on the author, and a conclusion.

- It has a *focus*: his anxiety about relationships.

- It has *proof*: the story of his conversation with a girl. Again, focused narrative development has made the proof vivid.

- It is short, to the point, and memorable. It is interesting without being grand, noble, or cosmic.

- The style, like the story, is simple — short sentences and simple words. A bit of real dialogue adds immediacy.

- It coordinates and enriches an application full of academic achievements and high scores and grades. It is information definitely not found elsewhere in the application.

Sample 4

"You may write about anything …." — Yale

It has come to my attention that our nation, and nations like ours, have long been plagued by a mysterious occurrence, an occurrence that is as perplexing as it is frustrating, "The Orphan Sock Enigma;" i.e., the constant disappearance of individual socks during the laundering process. It is a problem familiar to all of us, and also one to which we have unwillingly admitted defeat [sic].

I recently resolved to find an explanation. (In the grand tradition of science, I refused to be discouraged by the basic irrelevance of my cause.)

First, to verify that the problem exists, experimental and control loads of laundry were completely processed (put through the washer and dryer). In the experimental load (load with socks), by the end of the process, some socks were lost. But in the control load (load without socks), no socks were lost. Thus, the problem was verified.

Then, the actual experiment was done. In four separate trials, a number of socks (ten socks, or five pairs) were put through a normal drying cycle. The types of socks tested were selected by the highly accurate Harvey-Allman Principle Hierarchy and Zero Alternative Reduction Dimension (HAP-HAZARD).

The mass of the total load was measured prior to processing. Upon completion of the cycle, the mass of the remaining load plus the lint collected was also measured. In addition, the temperature of a running, empty dryer was measured, as was the temperature of a running, full dryer during the cycle. A table of data follows.

TRIAL #	#1	#2	#3	#4
Initial Mass 10 socks	265g	270g	276g	261g
Final Mass remaining socks and lint	261g	266g	271g	256g
Temp. running, empty dryer	65.56°C	65.56°C	65.56°C	65.56°C
Temp. running, dryer with socks	70.56°C	70.56°C	71.56°C	71.56°C
Net change in mass	4.0g	4.0g	5.0g	5.0g
Net change in temp.	5.0°C	5.0°C	6.25°C	6.25°C

In each and every trial, one or two of the socks were lost (each from a different pair). More importantly, in each and every trial, there was a net loss of mass and also a net increase in temperature. Through the use of Einstein's equation for mass-energy equivalence, E=mc2, the net loss of mass was accounted for by the net increase in temperature. All the evidence clearly pointed to one conclusion: all the socks that had been disappearing in countries all over the world had been directly converted to energy (or that there was something seriously wrong with my dryer).

It seems that the reaction can be controlled by the presence of different numbers of fabric softening sheets, similar to the effect of control rods in a nuclear reactor. In light of these discoveries, my house is now completely powered by a "Sock Reactor."

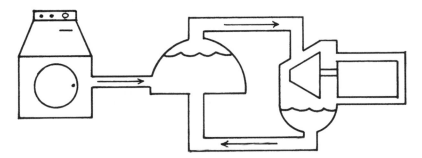

Fig. 1. Simplified Diagram of a "Sock Reactor"

I estimate that just a few "Sock Reactors" could supply power to a city the size of Chicago with zero danger (provided a good supply of fabric softening sheets is on hand). This is because one hundred percent of the mass is completely converted into energy safely, easily, and without leaving any of that unsightly radioactive waste common to those other name brand reactors.

Originally, I had hoped to keep knowledge of this discovery fairly restricted, but I fear that word has leaked out. I have reason to believe there is a merger planned between Interwoven Hosiery and General Power's nuclear division.

Although I have not been able to explain why only one sock out of a pair can be converted, it appears to in some way relate to a black hole, a time warp, and static cling.

Albert Einstein, the man who first discovered the mass-energy equivalence, never wore socks. I think that just about says it all.

Things to Notice About This Essay

- It's about an issue … not a serious one, but still an issue.

- It's written in essay form. It has an introduction, several paragraphs of proof, and a clear conclusion. However, it's also a creative piece that is not easily translatable into a formula and not easily duplicable by another writer.

- It has a *focus*: the "Orphan Sock Enigma."

- It is specific: the problem, the research, the chart and figure make it real and vivid. The author clearly knows how to plan, run, and record a scientific study, as well as how to spoof one.

- It presents a good picture of the writer, his interest in science, his imagination and humor, how extensively he thinks about life, and how well he can write.

- It is long. A humor piece is always an option but it should be tight, focused and (if there is one) within the word limit. The next draft might end with the Sock Reactor drawing.

Sample 5

"Your Space is your opportunity to allow the Committee on Admission to learn something about you that you have not addressed in another section of the application." — Vassar College

"I'm so bad at this," she said, shaking her red-orange hair. Michaela was standing in the middle of the soccer field holding a ball in her hands. She was trying to juggle it off her thighs, but couldn't do it more than three times in a row.

"No, you're not," I said. "Lots of the other kids are having trouble too."

She shook her head again. Without even noticing the other kids scattering after their balls as if they were trying to capture little runaway pets, she stuck out her bottom lip.

"Listen Michaela," I said, "When I was your age, I couldn't even juggle the soccer ball, let alone juggle it three times."

"But you can juggle it like a thousand times now, and I can't even get to four. It's not fair," she said.

Michaela pounded her soccer ball onto the ground and sat down on it. Her elbows rested on her knees and her chin came down on her fists. I sat down next to her.

"Michaela, how old are you?'

"Ten," she said jutting her chin out slightly.

"Do you know how old I am?"

"No."

"I'm seventeen. I've had seven years to practice my juggling and to get better at it. That's all it takes, practice. All you have to do is try to juggle the ball five times every day, and more when you can do that. Eventually, you'll be able to juggle more than I can," I said, looking at her with conviction.

She was staring at the ground, pulling tufts of grass up and piling little haystacks on top of her cleats. I could tell she wasn't sure whether to believe me or not. I got up and went to help some of the other kids, to give her a chance to think. Helping them seemed to mix encouragement in equal parts with leaving them alone with the challenge. One of the boys had given up altogether and was sitting on his soccer ball trying to peel an orange he'd kept from snacktime. Our coach called the kids around. Michaela got up and pouted her soccer ball up to the rest of the group. Matthew ran up to me on his way to the group and handed me his orange.

"Will you peel this for me?" he asked.

"Sure," I said.

I took the orange. The skin was slippery and slightly more yellow than orange. I thought about how hard it is to peel an orange. You have to dig your fingernail in far enough to get under the peel, but not so far as to puncture the flesh. Each piece is independent and seldom do you get a piece that makes the next one easier to peel. I poised the orange on my fingertips and tried to peel the first few pieces. Those are toughest; the skin is always the hardest and won't stay connected. I could feel bits of grainy peel under my fingernails. The kids started walking to lunch.

"Here you go," I said handing the orange back to Matthew, with a thick peel "pull tab" rising from the top. "I got it started, you should be able to take it from here."

Things to Notice About This Essay

- The author chooses a brief moment, a short pair of conversations in a single day of summer work — to convey a sense of her job, her style, and how she goes about encouraging others. It presents a writer who reflects on and connects her experiences.

- The applicant's talents as a writer ("pouted the ball") and as a teacher are clear from this story.

- The strategy is subtle, leaving most of the conclusions to the reader.

- The essay is very short, banking on the reader to get the point. Dialogue and visual detail (the ball, the orange peel) give immediacy to the story.

- This essay uses a bit of a high-risk strategy. Will the reader conclude the author is coming to college to play soccer or to study child development? The author is counting on the story to carry the meaning and omits the "From this I have learned …" conclusion. It's "her space" so anything goes. It works, because it's both short and vivid.

Sample 6

"Some students have a background or story that is so central to their identity that they believe their application would be incomplete without it. If this sounds like you, then please share your story." — Common Application Question

Determined as ever, I led my parents through the train station in the direction indicated by the lady at the ticket counter. My nine-year old legs struggled to keep up as we crossed the tracks and headed down a dreary hallway to a door marked "vedlikehold." I hoped that meant "lost and found" in Norwegian.

This was the moment of truth. We had searched everywhere. This was our last stop. As the door swung open, my eyes tried to focus through my last few tears and the cigarette smoke that hung heavy in the room. I looked past the chain-smoking attendants to a wall of dusty shelves stacked with forgotten umbrellas, cell phones, and briefcases. There he was, in all his purple and green glory, staring back at me with his black button eyes.

It was as though the ceiling bulb was a spotlight shining on my Barney the Dinosaur and the railway station's public address system was broadcasting Handel's "Hallelujah Chorus." This may seem like a hyperbole, but to an ecstatic little girl suddenly reunited with the best friend she thought was lost forever, it seemed like a miracle.

Why write about a lost stuffed animal, an embarrassing one at that, in a college essay? I think my ongoing relationship with Barney reflects much about who I am and who I want to become. For almost as long as I have loved Barney, I have wanted to care for children "when I grow up." Admittedly, my interests have evolved over time from a cast technician (after a broken arm), to a pediatric nurse (after an operation and several hospitalizations), to my determination to become a pediatrician — one who will never lose touch with a child's perspective on the world.

My work in Tanzania this past summer reinforced the need for adults who care for children to think like kids. The lead doctor on our medical outreach project, a stern man who had clearly lost his childhood innocence, failed to adequately explain the difference between the tubes of toothpaste and tubes of anti-fungal cream we were distributing to children in a remote Maasai village. I watched with horror as the kids enthusiastically squeezed the anti-fungal cream onto their brand new toothbrushes. Struggling to overcome the language barrier, I called upon years of expert charades-playing as I tried to pantomime the proper use of each medicine. This experience made it very clear to me that in order to truly help children, it is often necessary to think like a child. I hope to never lose this skill.

I am no longer that elated nine-year old at the Bergen train station clutching Barney with glee, but Barney will be coming to college with me. While I am eager for the intellectual and emotional challenges of college, I like the idea that Barney will be there to ground me in the security of my childhood. I hope to grow into an adult who will never lose her link with that past, who will one day help provide that sense of security to her patients, especially to those children who might not have parents willing or able to tromp through a remote train station in a faraway land in search of a lost, dearly-loved stuffed animal.

Things to Notice About This Essay

- The story is well-constructed, using a childhood recollection as the frame for a claim about how to communicate with diverse groups of people.

- The body of the essay traces an interest from an early broken arm to a summer volunteer trip to Africa. The evidence of her claim is a vivid story about toothpaste and charades.

- Paragraph three is probably dispensable. The emotional reunion has been made vivid in the "showing" of paragraph 1 and 2, and we don't need that extra "telling."

- The author addresses the reader directly and by setting up the question "Why write about a lost stuffed animal — in a college essay?" she transitions to why Barney is a useful lens through which to see and understand her.

- This toothpaste story is the most interesting part of the essay and carries all the important themes: her interest in becoming a pediatrician, her idea about retaining a child's point of view, her "can-do" attitude and determination, her creativity. A second draft might eliminate Barney (it was long ago) and begin at paragraph 5 ("My work in Tanzania this past summer …"). This would provide space in which to explore that one story more deeply. Why was no one able to explain the use of the medicines in the local language? Was the presiding doctor's stern style a serious drawback to the project's success? What actions did the author take after this event to avert other confusions? Did she have (or make) opportunities to share ways to improve the program?

- Notice the general flexibility of the Common Application questions. This essay could, with only a few adjustments, be about a failure or a transition to adulthood in Tanzania.

Sample 7

"Please tell us something about yourself, your experiences, or activities that you believe would reflect positively on your ability to succeed at Penn State."

> I used to be a pretty deep guy. I watched foreign films, read
> Nietzsche, and stayed up all night "contemplating jazz." I was Jack

Kerouac living in a fire hut on top of Desolation Peak. I was Gary Snyder seeking enlightenment in a Buddhist monastery in Thailand. I was Ken Kesey, Jimi Hendrix, and Timothy Leary all rolled up in one gigantic mess of pseudo-intellectual, adolescent, fancy boarding school beat poet wannabe. I was a moron.

I blew off my schoolwork not because I was lazy, but because I thought that schoolwork was shallow, too insignificant for me, the vivacious intellectual, the dharma bum, the Zen lunatic wanderer. How could my teachers expect me to do their homework, when life around me was all so futile, so meaningless? I was sure that I was a tortured soul destined to lead a life full of angst and pain.

That was last fall, more than a year ago now. In February of last year, I left my hipster friends and their coffeehouse conversations behind, to move back to the suburbs of Philadelphia and my conservative, unhip public high school. Suburban Philadelphia is not the easiest place in the world to be sixties cool and stylish. There aren't many smoke-filled coffeehouses or hippie wanderers. It's clean here, upper middle class — you know, the SUV's, Saturday evening Mass, Panera Bread for dinner. I came back to Philadelphia because it isn't all that "hip," because there is nothing "profound" to do. I came home to get myself together. It was time to grow up.

I'm not as cool as I used to be. Last weekend, I watched *Downton Abbey* with my mom, collected some weather data for a chemistry project, and had a tea party with my little sister. I've been spending time with the people I met in my high school production of *Arsenic and Old Lace*, too. I feel balanced; I feel like myself. I no longer want to tend bar in Tangiers or meditate in Sri Lanka ... all right, maybe I do, but not right now. For so long, I wanted to be other people, to be a cultural icon, a legend in my own time. But in reality, I'm nothing like Keith Richards. Honestly, I'm a little scared of sex and drugs. I worry about pimples, whether my parents are still happily married, where I'm going to be next year.

I came home, I grew up, I got my life back together. I'm still trying to find a balance, but I no longer feel like a reckless child. I was sure that

I could get away from myself by just pretending that I was someone else. But right now, I'm not looking to be "on the road." I'm pretty happy being right where I am.

Things to Notice About This Essay

- The story this writer tells seems sincere. It explains things from his transcript: a change of schools, improving grades.

- The essay expects the reader to know all the references here to people (Gary Snyder, Keith Richards) and literature (*On the Road, The Dharma Bums*, the line from poet Allen Ginsberg about "contemplating jazz"). The writer has a real depth of knowledge, which is good, as long as he isn't expecting too much from the reader.

- The essay has a clear focus ("It was time to grow up"), extensive use of specifics and descriptive details, and a strong sense of a writer who has thought about his life experience. He makes a good case for himself as an interesting addition to Penn State.

- The essay doesn't follow a traditional organization pattern and there are a few liberties with word choice and spelling ("wannabe"). A bit of a "risk," this essay does match a writer who himself has taken chances. He tells *his story* with grace and conviction.

Sample 8

"Why Brown?" (200 word limit) — Brown University

As a seventeen year old, I don't yet have the experience or vision to know exactly what I want to accomplish. What I hope Brown will do for me is to broaden my base of knowledge with a solid liberal arts education. I would like to explore Drake's equation for extraterrestrial life while analyzing the similes in Virgil's Aeneid. Or maybe I could investigate the applications of integral calculus or the themes of self-sacrifice in Shakespeare. From the combination of courses I decide to take, I expect to find one or two true passions.

While I am working towards an academic concentration, I would like to focus my athletic efforts on swimming. At Washington High, my intense training in swimming is interrupted every winter by my commitment to the basketball team. I am confident that concentrating solely on swimming will enable me to improve my past performances and times. If I could post a University record at Blodgett Pool and also find those one or two academic passions, I will have attained what I want. And I am hopeful that in combining and completing these goals, I will have given something back to the school.

Things to Notice About This Essay

- The suggested word-count has been a guide here. This answer is brief but a good match for the 200-word count limit set by the application.

- The writer's use of specific topics from a liberal arts curriculum suggests that she has thought about what's going to go on in college (Drake, Virgil, calculus, Shakespeare) and specifically the breadth of program Brown encourages. Weaker sentences are those lacking specifics (Sentence 2: "broaden my base of knowledge with a solid liberal arts education." Sentence 10: "combining and completing these goals, I will have given something back to the school").

- The writer is honest about her plans and her inability to predict a future four years away. But she is also positive about what she isn't sure of, emphasizing the future possibilities rather than her indecision. It's not a great match for an engineering school perhaps, but for Brown, which wants the student to be an "architect of your own education," it's not a surprise.

- It's wise to show a familiarity with the buildings and programs of the school to which you're applying, but if you "recycle" an essay like this one, be sure to proofread carefully. Blodgett Pool is at Harvard.

Sample 9

"Discuss an accomplishment or event, formal or informal, that marked your transition from childhood to adulthood within your culture, community, or family." — Common Application Question

I knew I was going to Pittsburgh to play in a tournament. I didn't know I would be visiting Houston, Pennsylvania between matches. A rural suburb twenty miles outside the city's industrial hub, Houston is my father's hometown.

His family, he says, was "dirt poor" and barely able to sustain the house we found still standing — tired of living, it seemed, and shedding its blue paint. My father pointed to a street corner blanketed with scattered sections of a local paper: "It was there ... right there ... where I stood and looked around me and saw that my future was contained in this town. It was painful to think of leaving. That street corner was the center of my universe." My father was the first person in his family — the first person in the little mining town — to go to college.

As my father drove me along the unpaved back roads, he tried to find messages and axioms in the half-century old tale, but they did not answer the chain of questions jerked along by my consciousness: *How did he get out? Why did he come back? Why did he want to bring me here? Can I be as proud of my life as he is of his? What do I have to accomplish to gain such satisfaction? Do I have to do it soon?*

His stories stacked on top of each other likes books on a desk. Each anecdote was another volume from his childhood and I was struggling to keep up with the reading. We passed the old house six times before he was ready to separate himself from Houston this time. The children playing outside the house tried to examine us through the tinted glass of our rented car and I shifted uncomfortably in my bucket seat. *What opportunities did they have? What would I do with mine?*

"Dad, these people are going to call the police if we keep circling the block."

Back at our hotel in Pittsburgh, I shouldered my racquet bag and followed my father up the staircase to our room. On each step, I tried to plant my foot exactly where he had put his.

Things to Notice About This Essay

- The organization is basically narrative. The writer's insights and reflections are incorporated into the story of her visit to Houston, Pennsylvania.

- The writer does not tell the reader what this experience means. In fact, her questions suggest she is still puzzling that out for herself. It's a risk, but she assumes we will figure out the connection between her father's experiences and her own, and see a transition from one view of the world to a more mature one. The italicized questions guide the reader in understanding the impact of this family experience.

- The writer supplies the details needed to create a picture of the place. The use of realistic dialogue adds credibility.

- The essay tells only a small story, but it reveals the writer's ability both to think about her own experiences and to understand the experiences of her father. No drama. But a convincing glimpse of a girl on her way to being a woman.

Sample 10

Work efficiently and do not reinvent the wheel for every application. The thinking that goes into choosing a vivid topic is substantial; a long reflection might be edited into a short response for a different application. Here, a fully developed essay becomes a 1,000 character paragraph.

As An Essay

Over the past 6 or 7 years, I have directed a neighborhood lawn mowing company. I began mowing our own lawn the summer after sixth grade, and gradually began to add clients to my list. Within three years, I had five weekly clients ($30 per lawn) and one employee — my brother. Charging $20–$40 per lawn, our profits doubled. This past summer, I earned roughly $1,040 to say nothing of my brother's payment. My profit increase is a little lopsided though, because I was able to work in the fall and late spring when I was in middle school. I've experienced the ups and downs of having an employee. I never had any real issues (although there were several times when a late start threw off our rotation). I've learned to keep track of payments on my own, and I created a simple accounting system. For the past four summers, I have been keeping my own books, making sure that I am paid correctly. Occasionally, I have had to collect missed payments. During one of my early summers, I had a client that was frequently on vacation. The client was not able to pay me right after my work, so I ended up losing profit. To avoid this, I began writing down the lawns I mowed each week, and then checking them off once I had been paid. While working for myself, rather than an employer, gave me the freedom to choose when I would work, I learned to plan to work around unpleasant weather or trips, vacations, and other commitments. With this freedom, however, came a great deal of responsibility. It could be very easy to miss one day of work and throw off the entire weekly cycle. I learned quickly that I had to consider the client's wishes, as well as my own personal schedule. I think that this knowledge has helped me with other jobs, particularly my first real paying job this summer. I learned that I had to make myself completely available during the work period, in case of schedule or shift changes or sudden needs to switch shifts. I sacrificed several weekend vacation trips for my work. I would definitely say that mowing lawns has helped me understand the need to be responsible and methodical, steady and constantly available, and not just in work. I apply this idea to my school life, as well. As a high school senior, my days are filled with classes, sports practices, and extracurriculars, not to mention homework. With the college process in full motion now, I have needed to make time for all kinds of meetings, both college visits and with my college counselor. I have learned to realize that these meetings are of importance equal to other activities I have mentioned. Working for myself mowing lawns, I came to understand the importance of being flexible for school work and real work. I apply this now to days filled with classes, sports practices, extracurriculars, and homework.

The Revision

~~Over the past 6 or 7 years, I have directed a neighborhood lawn mowing company.~~ I began mowing ~~our own lawn for~~ my parents' lawn the summer after ~~6~~sixth grade, and now have ~~gradually began to add clients to my list. Within three years, I had~~ five weekly clients ($30 per lawn) and one employee — my brother. ~~Charging $20-$40 per lawn, our profits doubled.~~ This ~~past~~ summer, I earned ~~roughly~~ $1040, (brother $ 656). ~~to say nothing of my brother's payment. My profit increase is a little lopsided though, because I was able to work in the fall and late spring when I was in middle school.~~ I've experienced the ups and downs of having an employee (the occasional ~~. I never had any real issues; although there were several times when a~~ late start ~~threw off our rotation~~) and~~.~~ I've ~~I~~ developed ~~learned to keep track of payments~~ my own ~~made, and I created a simple~~ accounting system. ~~For the past four summers, I have been keeping my own books, making sure that I am paid correctly. Occasionally, I have had to collect missed payments. During one of my early summers, I had a client that was frequently on vacation. The client was not able to pay me right after my work, so I ended up losing profit. To avoid this, I began writing down the lawns I mowed each week, and then checking them off once I had been paid.~~ While working for myself~~, rather than an employer, gave me the~~ frees me~~dom~~ to choose when I ~~would~~ work, working ~~. I learned to plan to work~~ around unpleasant weather or trips~~, vacations, and other commitments~~ can be tricky. ~~With this freedom, however, came a great deal of responsibility. It could be very easy to~~ One missed day ~~of work and~~ throws off the entire weekly cycle. ~~I learned quickly that~~ I have~~d~~ to consider the client's wishes, too.~~as well as my own personal schedule.~~ T~~I~~ think that ~~t~~his knowledge has helped me with other jobs, like ~~particularly~~ my first boat club ~~real~~

~~paying~~ job this summer. I ~~learned that I had to~~ mad~~k~~e myself completely available during the work period, in case of schedule or shift changes ~~or sudden needs to switch shifts.~~ and ~~I~~ sacrificed several weekend vacations ~~trips~~ for my work. ~~I would definitely say that~~ M~~m~~owing lawns has helped me ~~understand the need~~ to be responsible and methodical, steady and ~~constantly available, and not just in work. I apply this idea to my school life, as well. As a high school senior, my days are filled with classes, sports practices, and extracurriculars, not to mention homework. With the college process in full motion now, I have needed to make time for all kinds of meetings, both college visits and with my college counselor. I have learned to realize that these meetings are of equal importance to my life as the other activities I have mentioned. Working for myself mowing lawns, I came to understand the importance of being~~ flexible. ~~le for school work and real work.~~ I apply this now to days filled with classes, sports practices, extracurriculars, and homework.

As a Paragraph

I began mowing my parents' lawn the summer after 6th grade, and now have five weekly clients ($30 per lawn) and one employee — my brother. This summer, I earned $1,040 (brother $656). I've experienced the ups and downs of having an employee (the occasional late start) and I've developed my own accounting system. While working for myself frees me to choose when I work, working around unpleasant weather or trips can be tricky. One missed day throws off the entire weekly cycle. I have to consider the client's wishes, too. This has helped me with other jobs, like my first boat club job this summer. I made myself completely available during the work period, in case of schedule or shift changes, and sacrificed several weekend vacations for my work. Mowing lawns has helped me be responsible and methodical, steady and flexible. I apply this now to days filled with classes, sports practices, extracurriculars, and homework.

Things to Notice About This Essay

- This is a reasonable essay, well organized and detailed in describing the maturity he gained while running his own business.

- Ultimately, the author decided to use this for the state school application and wrote a different essay for his Common Application. But he was proud of his lawn-care business. Ruthless word reduction and lots of editing — his brother is now a quick reference and a parenthetical salary — fit this answer for several "activity" supplements

- This works in either format but is more like a cup of tea as the core essay and, as the paragraph, a shot of espresso. He made a good decision about the deployment of topics.

Sample 11

"Describe the world you come from — for example, your family, community or school — and tell us how your world has shaped your dreams and aspirations." — University of California

I come from a country that is economically oppressed, a country where speaking against the government could cost one his or her life. There is no established government. "Survival of the fittest" is the regulation that we live by. There is no law enforcement, no government to complain to, and no police to call to one's rescue when one is being robbed or attacked.

The average Haitian only completes high school if he or she is fortunate. There exist circumstances in which a student has to leave school to work to care for their family even though work opportunities are insufficient. Times get harder and more unbearable as days go by. People get killed for no fixed reason, food becomes limited, and more and more children are getting ill.

My family consisted of eight people, all living on the second floor of a three-story house that included only two bedrooms. My sister and I slept in the same bed and in the same bedroom as my mother and two aunts. Paying the rent was difficult, for no one in the family was employed.

My grandmother left for the United States in 1997 when I was two years old. Since her arrival in America, she has stayed at someone's house. She was not yet familiar with the language, so it was difficult for her to find a job. She worked as a seamstress at home where she would make dresses for people and get paid, but that was not enough to establish her goal, which was to get her family here in America. Later, she worked as a housekeeper for five years; however, that job was also not sufficient. Knowing that she had children and grandchildren back in her native country, my grandma was determined to do everything in her power to take us out of our misery and bring us here to the land of opportunity.

Although my grandmother was going through harsh and difficult times, like finding transportation for work back and forth in the terrible weather, not being able to communicate with others, or being kicked out, she never forgot about us in Haiti. She would pay our house rent and send money for our schooling and for food. Also she filed for citizenship on our account, so it could be a quicker process of coming to the United States. After seven long years we were able to come. November 28, 2004 was such an emotional and joyous day for the entire Joseph family.

There is nothing more that I want in this world than to thank my grandmother and truly show her how important she is to me. She is an exceptional, strong, and independent woman. As of now I am doing my best to attend a four-year college. My love for the community has influenced my career choice. I have resolved in my heart that no matter what I do I must be capable of providing assistance for others. Caring for others has always been my passion and going into a medical field or health profession is what I am striving for. The best way I see fit to give back to a community that has given so much to me is by becoming a nurse practitioner. Hopefully, I will be my grandmother's first grandchild to successfully graduate college. Being able to accomplish all my scholastic goals, I believe, I will not only honor my grandmother but also show her my appreciation for all the hard work she has done for me.

Things to Notice About This Essay

- A strong opening sentence makes us want to keep reading.

- The essay describes the author's family and from this the reader can derive a sense of the author's determination and aspirations.

- The essay is well organized, based on the chronology of her grandmother's story, and makes a clear connection between the events of the author's life and her future plans.

- We learn about the grandmother's generosity, commitment, and love; we want to know more about the author of this essay herself. How did *she* come to the United States? When did *she* learn English? How does *she* live now?

- Is there some evidence that proves that the grandmother's actions have already affected the author's life? Is there community service or a supporting action within the writer's daily life that can serve as proof for the claim that her grandmother has inspired her? Her own actions (not her planned future) are the missing pieces in this narration.

- University of California offers a 1,000-word limit for its two essays, so there is space here to add the information suggested above.

Sample 12

"Recount an incident or time when you experienced failure. How did it affect you, and what lessons did you learn? — Common Application Question

View your actions and aspirations simply as a reflection of your brother's. Realize the unfairness of it all: your sibling has and always will be better than you. Feel the urge to reach across the dinner table and punch him in the face as he discusses the "dire state of our economy" and how the works of Hegel are fundamentally flawed. Clench your fists in frustration as you simply ponder how tough your day was. There is nothing you can do to alter your mindset of inferiority towards your brother.

Believe that you can't possibly compete with your brother's flawless academic achievements. Grimace when he receives an SAT score of 2260. Spend at least four hours a night on homework; observe as your brother seems to finish in minutes. He receives straight A's. Curse angrily when you see him racing around campus, his Acceptance Letter clutched tightly in his hand. Interpret the smile on his face as an indication that you can't achieve what he did. Gasp as he lectures the family on the pros and cons of socialism. Be angry knowing that, although you try much harder, he achieves much more and often without effort. Sense the futility of a Physics project as you realize that your brother could make it much better. Your physics teacher quickly dismisses your final project as 'OK"; you believed it was a masterpiece.

Witness an extremely odd and rare occurrence. Your brother just failed his driving test. He turned left on a red light. Remember that, like you, he's colorblind. Realize that he has failed something significant. He is not invincible. Gain confidence. Know that you yourself possess qualities which your wicked smart brother doesn't. Comprehend that perhaps you've been improved both as a scholar and a person because of the competition and expectation.

Sit at the table with your family. Listen to the chatter about the day. Eye your brother. Prepare yourself for the barrage of useless facts that you know he is about to deliver. Wait patiently for the upcoming lesson about *The Heart of Darkness*, or the complex principles behind Darwinism.

He begins, "So guys, did you know that Darwinism is actually a form of —."

"You know what, Percy, I'd prefer to talk about something *interesting* for a change. As much as I'm sure we'd all love to immerse ourselves in the world of Darwin, let's not." Look around at your family members, your eyes resting on Percy. Begin giggling. Attempt an insincere apology, "Sorry, Perc, you're just such a damn *nerd*!"

Things to Notice About This Essay

- The style of the essay is arresting. Written in the imperative mode (it's all commands), the author tells an emotional story with balance and neutrality.

- The events are simple and the theme of jealousy is human and believable.

- The essay reveals an introspective author, a writer with a flair for style and creativity.

- Is the topic too negative? Will admission readers object to the author's anger and snarky sense of humor? Honesty and the realism of the details should overcome these issues.

- Length might be a bit of a problem…this works as long as the author doesn't belabor the story. The left turn arrives just in time. Should he do more with his assertion that this event has changed his attitude toward his brother? No. Sibling rivalry lasts forever.

- A "failure" prompt can be tricky. Not because we don't all fail (we do) but because it's tempting to excuse the failure and write mostly about subsequent success. If you choose a question like this, 80% should be a strong and vivid presentation of how you made a mess of something. Then add just a thin layer of redemption at the end. As above.

Sample 13

"Alumna and writer Anna Quindlen says that she 'majored in unafraid' at Barnard. Tell us about a time when you majored in unafraid."

In fourth grade, my teacher handed me a "Mad Minute" worksheet. We had sixty seconds to complete as many of the 50 multiplication problems as possible. This meant that we had 1.2 seconds for each problem. The first "Mad Minute" was the most traumatic. Eight years old, forty problems left, twenty seconds gone, nine times seven, sixty-four-no-three, thirty seconds gone, fourteen problems done, ten seconds left, twenty students done, eight years old, zero times anything, zero, zero seconds left, twenty-three students done, thirty problems left—time's up.

"I did forty-four," sang the curly haired girl on my left. "How many did *you* finish?"

"Twenty," I mumbled.

I came home from school that day convinced that I would never be able to multiply. Just before I threw in the towel on elementary school mathematics, however, my mother gave me a choice: I could resign myself to the idea that I would carry a calculator with me wherever I would go, or else I could practice multiplication to get my computational skills up to speed. She offered to sit with me for ten minutes each night before bed, quizzing me on multiplication flashcards. Although even today my idea of math is answering why six is afraid of seven (because seven ate nine), I do not give up. Anna Quindlen says that she "majored in unafraid" at Barnard. I majored in unafraid every time I took my multiplication flashcards out before bed in fourth grade. I still major in unafraid, every time I raise my hand in class to ask, "Can we go over number four again?"

Things to Notice About This Essay

- The author captures a moment from long ago as a lens on her claim that "I do not give up."

- She uses a clever irony in the opening paragraph — although she appears to be slow at math, her quick calculation of the time allotted to each problem in a Mad Minute suggests she's more than able to do the work.

- She makes a strong connection between a fourth-grade event and her adult willingness to ask questions and face criticism in order to understand completely whatever is under discussion.

- A bit of humor is always welcome ("seven ate nine").

- The space limit is 1,000 characters. She's close, but to meet the requirement, she should reduce the description of her flash-card review rather than taking anything away from the Mad Minute or the connection to her current learning style.

- This short narrative makes a convincing connection to the kind of student Barnard (or any other college) hopes to enroll.

Sample 14

Many of the comments above have urged the authors to show not tell, i.e., to be more specific and more vivid. Here's a sample meant to show how to revise a reasonable draft for "Please briefly elaborate on one of your extracurricular activities" (1,000 characters) for a faster start and a more in-depth treatment.

In Foundations, our youth group at Old Saint Patrick's church, everyone contributes, sharing faith and the love we have for helping others. About 50 high-schoolers participate in Sunday mass — choir, ushers, the offeratory procession, or as Eucharistic ministers. I have done the last three. Our bonding has included an overnight lock-in, a retreat, and Sunday meetings. Last year's theme was "taking off your mask." We talked about peer influence, high school situations, and listening to yourself. This year, "being a revolution," we do by community service. We volunteered at a bike repair shop, sold pumpkins for Halloween, and made and sold Advent candles, raising raised money for last summer's service trip to Nicaragua. The Foundation spirit came together in the village of Cusmapa, where we American teenagers supported the world of the Fabretto Foundation by doing construction and maintenance on the schoolhouses, but also by teaching and playing with the Nicaraguan children.

Things to Notice About This Essay

- The essay focuses on a church youth group and the many activities the author has been involved in there.

- There are useful details about the bike repair shop, the pumpkins, and the candles. It would be interesting to know how much money was raised.

- Small spelling and proofreading errors need attention: "offeratory," "raising raised."

- The trip to Nicaragua is presented as the culmination of the Foundation spirit but the author has run out of characters by the time she gets to that topic. Her best strategy is to compress the preliminary details. Once she's taken us all the way to Nicaragua, we want to dwell there a little.

- With a tighter beginning, the author can give more detail and add some explanation of the importance of the Nicaragua experience for the group.

- That will take a little thinking but colleges like people who are willing to do a little thinking.

Revision—a work in progress:

Old Saint Patrick's youth group, Foundations, puts 50 high-schools in Sunday mass as choir, ushers, the offertory procession, or Eucharistic minister (I have done the last 3) and our bonding has included lock-ins, retreats, and weekly meetings. We worked particularly hard last year selling pumpkins, Advent candles, and working in a bike repair shop to raise $2,000 for our trip to Cusmapa ...

The writer has liberated 600 characters for details and her insights about this trip. Carry on.

A Final Word: Insist on Yourself

I do not recommend any of these drafts to you as models. I present them as examples of the strengths (focus, proof, simple language, structure, vividness) and weaknesses (slow starts, wordiness, generalities, lack of support for claims about yourself, about a college, or about the impact of an event) that have been discussed throughout this book. It is irrelevant what schools these essays were written for or whether the applicants were accepted. And, in a funny sort of way, it's even irrelevant what the questions are. Remember McGrath's advice: "There is no one standard." Just your standard. As an important part of the overall performance and impression of an application, your essay can be lazy or it can work for you. A look at these samples should help you avoid the pitfalls, enjoy the variety, and end up with a connected, strong, and vivid "Tell us about yourself" presentation for colleges of your choice.

Toolbox: Quick Fixes for Procrastinators

Deadlines can be inspiring. It's not too late to do a great job. There's no reason you can't put together a winning essay in a few hours...you just need to start. Here are some jumpstart techniques to get fingers onto the keyboard. And remember, "Begun is half-done."

Whatever essay prompt is hovering there on your screen, there's a good chance it is asking you to focus on an event, decision, or experience and explain its importance. Try one or more of the following ideas and see which one "has legs" for you. Just do it. There's no right answer here. Just your answer.

1. Bang out a little paragraph on your team or your job or the chorus trip. (Note: the best choice is something you've done over a fairly long period of time, not a two-week trip or a one-hour community service event.) Set the timer for 15 minutes and get that done. Describe your involvement and add four or five sentences about why it was or is important to you. Revise those "importance" sentences so they say more than "from this I have learned to work with others." There...a short essay done! Several schools ask for this kind of activities paragraph.

2. Look around your room. Pick three things you plan to take to college with you (or wish you could). Write a sentence for each that explains why that poster, that chunk of rock, that photograph matters to you. Then see if one of these things might be the beginning of an essay about you and an event or experience that illuminates you.

3. Write a letter to your future roommate introducing yourself. If you can relax and compose this as a real letter, you will have begun the "Tell us about yourself" process in an effective and useful way. And you might even have finished your essay as this is the question on several schools' applications.

4. Run through your Facebook albums. What images stand out in your mind? What events were depicted? Try to find a thread of interest — a renewed friendship, a magic place, a person who keeps showing up at the important moments. What evidence in your life today proves the influence of that person or place? These ideas fit well with several application questions.

5. Go find a parent. Ask what your strengths and talents are. Ask what "kind" of person you are. What characteristics and talents should you mention that you've overlooked. However you do it, don't fail to exploit

the knowledge of a person who's spent 17 years with you (and who really likes you).

6. Is there time to talk to your guidance counselor, a favorite teacher, or a coach? Ask them where they think you should go to college and why they chose that place. Ask them what it is they think you contribute to a group; then think about a specific time when that was evident in class or on your team.

7. Go back to any journal or portfolio assignment you've done for school. How have you changed since you did this work? Does it still interest you? If yes, consider talking about the assignment (for an example of how this might work, see the *zea mays* essay in Chapter 5). If not, even better — a change of heart, an experience of growth and transition, waits to be described.

8. Think of something you used to believe and don't believe anymore, something you thought was true but turned out to be false — write a few sentences about before and after and what caused the change. Does this seem to reflect your thoughtfulness and curiosity? A central story in your life? A transition from childhood? (Don't write about Santa Claus.)

If the supplement is a "Why us?" question, begin with the academic style and offerings of the college. Other factors — location, teams, housing options — come last. Be specific, be knowledgeable, and be sure your answer could never be used for any school other than the one for which you are drafting it.

If there's time, ask someone you like — someone who will give you a straight answer and knows you well — to read the essay and tell you what they learned about you from reading it. If they've only learned you play soccer or like French, for example, then start over. Make your essay work for you; it needs to enrich or *add* to your application.

Finally, remember colleges are interested in your mind more than your biography. What has happened to you doesn't matter much. What matters is what you've thought about what has happened to you. Show the reader an event, but only for the purpose of making it revealing and full of thoughtfulness. Think of what your application won't show about your mind and your heart if it's just grades and numbers; then try to find an event that will illuminate that mind and that heart. Write it, look it over, tighten it up for clarity, upload it, and submit. Get on with the life you are living and trust the process. You've done your part; they'll do theirs.

Suggested Reading

Note: most of these titles are also available as eBooks.

Barnet, Sylvan, Pat Bellanca, and Marcia Stubbs. *A Short Guide to College Writing*. 11th ed. New York: Pearson, 2014.

Corbett, Edward P. J., and Sheryl L. Finkle. *The Little English Handbook: Choices and Conventions*. 8th ed. New York: Longman, 2010.

Gibaldi, Joseph. *MLA Handbook for Writers of Research Papers*. 7th ed. New York: Modern Language Association, 2009.

Hacker, Diana and Nancy Sommers. *A Writer's Reference*. 6th ed. Boston: Bedford Books, 2010.

Strunk, William, and E. B. White. *The Elements of Style*. 4th ed. New York: Longman, 1999.

Trimble, John. *Writing with Style: Conversations on the Art of Writing*. 3rd ed. New York: Longman, 2010.

Zinsser, William. *On Writing Well*. New York: Harper Perennial, 2006.

Index